A Heart

For God

*A Biblical Guide to Experiencing
True Heart Transformation*

John Coblentz

Ridgeway Publishing
Medina, New York

A HEART FOR GOD

For additional copies
please visit your local
bookstore or contact:

Ridgeway Publishing
3129 Fruit Avenue
Medina, NY 14103
ph: 888.822.7894
fax: 585.798.9016

Printed in the United States of America

Introduction

Man was created in the image of God. Considering this, the heart is a marvelous thing. It is created by God, for God. It has longings and desires and out of those man responds. Our heart was designed to serve God.

But man is born in a fallen world with a fallen heart making it "deceitful above all things and desperately wicked. Who can know it?" Jeremiah 17:9

Sin damages our hearts, deadens our conscience, darkens our understanding and mind and warps our desires. It enslaves the will, clouds our judgment and alienates us from God.

But thanks be to God for Jesus Christ and the power of His atoning blood. The Spirit of God and the Word of God serve as a spotlight to search our hearts to reveal lies we believe about ourselves and the sinfulness of our carnal nature.

Then there is cleansing. Through repentance, confession, acquaintance and fellowship with God, the heart is changed and recreated in the likeness of Him who loved and died for us. Now we have a new and clean heart with new desires and longings. One that is being changed into the same image from glory to glory even as by the Spirit of the Lord. Through having a love for truth and experiencing God's love in our hearts we can have a Heart For God.

This book is written for those who love light and are willing to expose their hearts to God and man. It is written on a scriptural basis with clear outlines and easy reading style for the sincere child of God. The reader will be challenged, inspired, instructed and changed into a vessel that is fit to bring glory and honor to Christ's kingdom. May we ever be inspired to have a Heart For God.

—Aaron Beachy

Publisher's Note

You will notice this book reads different than some of the author's other books you may have read. That is because this is a transcription of a series of talks that were given at a seminar. Nevertheless, it is written in an easy-to-read format and you will be blessed by the message.

—Norman MIller

Table of Contents

Chapter 1

Functions of the Heart

Throughout the Bible, we regularly see God focusing His attention on the heart of man. We look on the outward appearance—and we easily make judgments about the heart—but only God can look accurately at the heart.

As you go through these sessions on the heart, God will be speaking to you, and ideas will form in your mind. That is how God made us. We think, we reason, we put things together, and we conclude. You will also feel things as you think about your life, your heart, and your experiences. And you will be urged both from within and from the thoughts presented here to make decisions based on what you are learning and feeling. May you experience the presence of God as you look further at your heart!

In the first part of this session, we will explore some of the major components of the heart.

The Mind

Let's think about our minds. We are thinking all the time. We have a continuous stream of thoughts—we never really stop thinking. In that thinking, we form ideas. What we think about tends to be the material by which we form our ideas. It's important that we think on good things to form good ideas. From our ideas, then, we develop a whole system of thinking based on the thoughts that are going through our mind.

Isn't this circular reasoning?

Does God care about what's happening in your mind? Does He care about the stream of thoughts that travel through your mind continually? If you were to take the stream of thoughts that went through your mind today—over the last twenty-four hours—were they pleasing to God? The psalmist says, "Let the words of my mouth, and the meditation of my heart be acceptable in thy sight" (Psalm 19:14). What you are thinking about is forming the ideas by which you live. We only fool ourselves if we suppose we can think trash all day and not have trashy minds. Does God care about the mind? He certainly does.

The Will

Let's shift our focus now to the will—another component of the heart. Do you know that you are regularly using your will just like you are regularly using your mind? You make decisions all through the day. Right along with the constant stream of thoughts going through your mind is this constant stream of decisions. You turned left, you turned right, you went straight ahead, you stopped, you pondered, you said, "Oh, I forgot," you turned around and went back. Think of all the decisions you made today. You don't just "happen" to be some place at any given time in a day. You got there by a process of decisions. If you are a member of a church, you became a member through a process of decisions. We are where we are at any point in our lives as a result of decisions. They continually direct our lives. *[handwritten: Is this true?]*

Sometimes people will say weird things about how they got where they are. They sin, for example, and they explain it something like this:

"All at once I found myself at a bar."

No, you didn't. You made decisions that took you there.

Or, "All at once I just found myself in a compromising position with a woman."

No, you didn't. You made decisions that led you there. *[handwritten: Is this always true? what about Joseph?]*

We are continuously making decisions. God knows the thought and intents of our hearts. He knows those decisions. He knows the junctions where we stood in thought and then decided to walk this way instead of that way. God knows all that is going on in the heart of man.

Desires and Wishes

Often our decisions are pushed along by our desires and wishes—what we want.

Think about what directs your decisions. No doubt it is partly your thoughts and ideas and the conclusions you come to, but it is also your wants and desires and the things you purpose.

If you are a young man, have you ever considered what kind of an old man you want to be? Or young ladies, what kind of old lady would you like to be? Maybe you think, "I don't want to ever be an old man or old lady."

what about an 11th hour convert?

I'm sorry, it's coming. Whatever kind of person you will be in old age will be the product of the lifetime of choices you have made. It is something that is going on continually in your heart. You don't just happen to get to be the kind of person you are. It involves the kinds of thoughts you put into your mind. And it involves the choices you make with your will.

Function of the Will

When we talk about choices, wishes, desires, and yearnings of our heart, we are talking about how the will functions. That's where we decide things. That's where we make commitments. Those are function of the will.

Daniel, at one point in his life, purposed in his heart that some things he would not do. He had come to that settled conclusion. It was the exercise of his will. It was a resolve he made.

How do commitments stabilize us? Do they, for sure?

The little choices we make comprise the foundation for the bigger commitments we make in life—those commitments that stabilizes us. Some people have an unspoken commitment to their work. Some people have a commitment to their lust. They have made that commitment, and you cannot pull them away from that commitment. Our commitments determine how we live.

Emotion and Feelings

The third component of the heart is the feeling center. This part of our hearts could be called the push-pull part of us. What tends to push your will one way or the other? Did you ever notice how your emotions—your inner feelings—have a big part to play here? Sometimes, for example, you just don't feel like getting up in the morning. The feeling is just not there to push you out of bed. Then suddenly, you may realize it is past work time! You are urged by your new feelings at that point to say, "I'd better get up!"

It's good God gave us feelings. Some of us would never get anywhere if it weren't for a little fear in our hearts. Our feelings push us, urge us, pull us, and in many ways help us make decisions. *Somewhat contrary to popular Anabaptist opinion,*

Feelings have other functions as well.

Our feelings also serve as connectors. They help us to bond with others. The Scriptures tell us to "Rejoice with them that do rejoice, and weep with them that weep" (Romans 12:15). Do you know why? That bonds us together. You weep with somebody, and you become a soul partner. You have joined with that person at a deep level of your being. You can also bond with others when you share joy with them.

And so, our emotions serve a number of functions, but notice now: you are always feeling something through the day. And as with thoughts and decisions, the continuous stream of feelings turns into *How do you know it's not the other way* something bigger as it flows along. Feelings become *round?* dispositions and moods. Some people are regularly cheerful. Others just kind of pull you down because their disposition is glum.

Now, we have thought about three important components of the heart—the mind, the will, and the emotions. Here is an important consideration: They work as a unit rather than as separate components. In explaining them here, I have talked about them separately, but in human experience, they can't actually be separated. In reality when you think, you also feel. You're also likely making choices. When you decide, you are thinking. You are using your mind to evaluate and make those choices. The heart functions as a unit. We can draw lines in diagrams, but we really can't draw hard lines between choices and thoughts or between thoughts and feelings. Talking about them separately can be (helpful) for understanding them, but what is going on in our hearts is not three separate functions. *deceptive?*

The Heart Wears a Body

Did you know that your heart wears a body? Your body is walking around, but your heart is actually wearing it. That is, through your body your heart finds expression. Your heart is the core part of you, and it uses your body to find outlets for expression of the nature it has. Do you have a good heart or an evil heart? It is through your body that the nature of your heart will be made known. Your appearance, your actions, everything you do or say is coming out of your heart. What people see when they meet you is just what you are wearing on the outside. The real "you" is inside there. You are only wearing that body. You're wearing a face. You are expressing your heart on your face. What is your heart saying through your body? Your body is communicating the kind of heart you have. It is always saying who is in here.

Digging Deeper

When we find nasty words coming out of our mouth, we tend to think something like this: "Oh, I need to quit saying those nasty words." God wants to deal with the heart from which those words came. It won't work to wear a nice looking exterior if we don't do anything about the wickedness of our heart. The Scripture says, "The heart is deceitful above all things, and desperately wicked" (Jeremiah 17:9). That's why we need a heart change. But we tend to think, "I'll put a nice cover on this heart and then I'll be a nice person!" God says, "No, you've got to deal deeper than that."

Your words, your actions, your countenance, and your body are the expressions of your heart. The Scriptures are clear about these issues. In Romans 12:1 we read, "I beseech ye therefore, brethren, by the mercies of God, that ye present your bodies a living sacrifice." The word present means "to yield." We are to yield our bodies to God because before we knew God, we yielded our bodies to sin. Paul is saying we are to give our bodies over to God.

The Heart in God's Word

All through the Scriptures, we find references to the heart. Early on, we have a window into the heart of God. In Genesis 6:6 we read, "It repented the Lord that he had made man on the earth, and it grieved him at his heart." Why was this? Because God saw the hearts of people: "Every imagination of the thoughts of his heart was only evil continually" (Genesis 6:5). Here you have a description of how God feels about the condition of the human heart.

I think there are between 900 and 1000 references to the human heart in the Bible. God's eye is continually on the heart of man. We look on the outward appearance, but God looks on the heart (see 1 Samuel 16:7). God told Samuel this as He was selecting Israel's king.

How does the heart function?

What is the heart of man? Obviously the biblical writers were not talking about the physical organ. I find it interesting that different cultures use different internal organs to describe this internal part of man —this part of him that is deeper than his body. Some cultures refer to it as the liver or the bowels. However it is expressed, it is something deep within, a non-tangible part of man.

As I read other authors, I find that there is really not a clear agreement on exactly what the heart is. It must not be an easy thing to define. In a general way I think we all recognize that it's the non-material part of who we are. There's the physical, and there is the spiritual. We sometimes call it the inner person. The Scriptures use different terms for this inner part of man. In 2 Corinthians 4:16 we find the terms "the inner man" and "the outward man." Many times the word heart is used to describe that inner part of who we are.

One author says the heart refers to the motives. Others say that the heart is the feelings. You may have heard someone say, "That's a truth I know in my head, but I don't know it in my heart." When people say that, they usually mean they haven't been able to feel it. Other authors have described the heart as the will.

Human beings apparently conclude different things about the heart, but we need to remember that the Scriptures are the final authority. We have the privilege of coming to the Scriptures and absorbing and hearing what they have to say.

As I share my thoughts with you, my desire is to share scripturally. And I pray that what I share is more than just language, more than just ideas. My belief is that where God is loved and adored, He will be present. I want you to experience the presence of God so that He can speak from His heart to yours.

Keeping our hearts

The first nine chapters of the Book of Proverbs could be referred to as "father-to-son instructions." Over and over, you hear the writer saying, "My son.... My son...." Sometimes he uses it in the plural form: "Hear, ye children" (Proverbs 4:1). I'm not going to look at all those references, but let's look at several.

In Proverbs 1:10 Solomon says, "My son, if sinners entice thee, consent thou not."

In Chapter 4 he says in Verses 3 and 4, "For I was my father's son, tender and only beloved in the sight of my mother. He taught me also, and said unto me, Let thine heart retain my words: keep my commandments and live."

Verse 10: "Hear, O my son, and receive my sayings; and the years of thy life shall be many."

Verse 20: "My son, attend to my words; incline thine ear unto my sayings." The instructions this father is giving to his son are very important. He wants his son to pay attention to what he is saying.

Then in Verse 23 he says, "Keep thy heart with all diligence; for out of it are the issues of life." Guard your heart. Protect it. Give every effort to protect and keep your heart because out of it are the issues of life. The heart is the source. Some translations would say it is the wellspring—the spring or fountain from which we live. It is the source of all living.

The Scriptures talk about this in other places too. Jesus said in Matthew 12:34, "For out of the abundance of the heart the mouth speaketh." Our words—what we say—come from our hearts. Later Jesus says, "...for out of the heart proceed evil thoughts, murders, adulteries, fornications, thefts, false witness, blasphemies" (15:19). Those things are evil things coming out of the heart, but notice the references to thoughts and actions. This is simply illustrating what the proverb writer said many years before that. Out of the heart we speak, we think, we decide, we live, we do, and we act.

Because we live out of our hearts, we are urged to keep our hearts guarded and protected.

Why it is necessary?

In Matthew 12:34 Jesus says, "For out of the abundance of the heart the mouth speaketh." He goes on to say in verse 35, "A good man out of the good treasure of the heart bringeth forth good things: and an evil man out of the evil treasure bringeth forth evil things." What does that tell us? The character of the heart, the nature of the heart, the condition of the heart determines the character of the expression. The kind of heart you have will determine the kind of expression. What is in our hearts will come out in our words, actions, and thoughts.

If we have a good heart, then the things that come out of that heart will be good. Our actions will be good actions. Our thoughts will be good thoughts. Our words will be good words.

The opposite is true also. As Jesus said, evil expressions will come out of an evil heart. In Matthew 15:19, Jesus names numerous sinful actions that come out of a sinful heart—actions such as adultery, murder, and theft. What we need to understand is that the nature of a heart, the character of the heart, the kind of heart we have determines all that comes out of that heart.

In some ways, this can sound too simple because human beings can confuse the situation. Sometimes a person will say really nice things to cover an evil heart. So, it isn't quite as simple as it sounds to say that a person who says good things has a good heart and a person who says evil things has an evil heart. Sometimes what we see looks good, but actually it is a cover for what is bad.

There were times people criticized Jesus. There were times people criticized the prophets. They said, "What you're saying is bad!" In that case, their judgment was wrong. There were other times when Jesus was harsh with people who declared they had a good heart and actually were confusing onlookers by outwardly looking good. They talked so good. They had narrowed down goodness to something that could be measured. And they used their "measuring stick" on everyone else.

Jesus seemed to have harsher words for the people who put a good front on an evil heart, than for the people who were brought to Him as sinners. Some of those people who were sinners in the presence of Jesus repented. It's hard for a person who has confused good and evil to see the nature of what he is doing. It is especially hard when he thinks he is good but is actually using good to make a nice front. Only God can trace what is on the outside—our actions and words—to the heart accurately and completely.

We all are concerned about what is in the heart.

Somebody might say a nice thing about us, and we quickly wonder if it's really from the heart. Is that really what they meant? If we sense that a person is just saying something nice and we know good and well that's not what is in their heart, then their words are almost worse than if they would have told us what they actually think. Isn't that how we are?

Reading each other

Let's carry this point further. We "read" each other's words and actions to try to discern the heart. We are always evaluating and wondering why a person did this or that. I don't think it's necessarily wrong, but we are given some strong cautions. We don't have the clarity of God in seeing one another and so we're warned not to judge. At the same time, Jesus told us, "...by their fruits ye shall know them" (Matthew 7:20).

But let's come back to God again. Just after He talked about our words, Jesus said in Matthew 12:36, "Every idle word that men shall speak, they shall give account thereof in the day of judgment." Notice verse 37: "For by thy words thou shalt be justified, and by thy words thou shalt be condemned." What's that saying? God can look at anything we say and trace it perfectly to the heart. He knows if those words are actually good words, because He knows the heart. God can do that perfectly. We can't, so He gives us caution. It's not to say that we should not think about the heart or be unconcerned about the heart of other people, but we recognize that we can't fully see the heart.

More Functions of the Heart

Let's look more specifically at functions of the heart.

When I refer to the "function of the heart," I'm talking
about what the heart does. Here are some Scriptures
from the New Testament that refer to the heart:
"... think ye evil in your heart" (Matthew 9:4)
"... should understand with their heart" (Matthew
13:15)
"... love the Lord thy God with all thy heart"
(Matthew 22:37)
"... reasoning in their heart" (Mark 2:6)
"... shall not doubt in his heart" (Mark 11:23)
"... imaginations of their hearts" (Luke 1:51)
"... pondered these things in her heart" (Luke 2:19)
"... mused in their heart" (Luke 3:15)
"... slow of heart to believe" (Luke 24:32)
"... let not your heart be troubled, neither let it be
afraid" (John 14:1)
"... shall not doubt in his heart" (Mark 11:23)
"... imagination of their hearts" (Luke 1:51)
"... pondered them in her heart" (Luke 2:19)
"... mused in their hearts" (Luke 3:15)
"... our hearts burn within us" (Luke 24:32)
"... your heart shall rejoice" (Acts 2:26)
"... they were pricked in their heart" (Acts 2:37)
"... they were cut to the heart" (Acts 5:33 and 7:54)
"... with purpose of heart" (Acts 11:23)
"... to weep and break mine heart" (Acts 21:13)
"... lust of their own hearts" (Romans 1:24)
"... sorrow in my heart" (Romans 9:2)
"... believe in thine heart" (Romans 10:9)
"... harden not your heart" (Hebrews 3: 8)
"... evil heart of unbelief" (Hebrews 3:12)
"... thoughts and intents of the heart" (Hebrews
4:12)
As we look at these references to the heart, we are

trying to answer a question: What is the heart doing? How does it function?

As we read through these verses, the functions can be categorized into two general divisions: internal and expressive. They are internal when what is happening is inside the heart. They are expressive when something is coming out of the heart. On the one hand, we see things happening in the heart, and on the other hand, we see things coming out of the heart.

How does this heart within us work?

In the Heart

Let's explore the internal functions first.

Notice these verses: "Daniel purposed in his heart" (Daniel 1:8). That was something that happened internally. He did something in his heart. Now, it affected his actions, but it was an internal resolve.

Psalm 19:14 says, "Let the words of my mouth and the meditations of my heart...." Meditations are things that are happening in the heart. Did you ever find yourself just sitting and meditating? Something was going on inside you—the meditating was happening in your heart.

In Psalm 55:4 we read, "My heart is sore pained within me." I don't know your heart. I don't know your life. But it is likely that somewhere you have pain. Some situation in your life is giving you sorrow. A relationship in your life could be giving you sorrow. I just had an e-mail from a lady whose husband left her, and she's in intense pain. He's living with another lady. His wife has several children and she's struggling and struggling and struggling with what to do. She has thoughts and questions like "How do I relate to my husband? Do I let him come home? He's living with this other lady, and she's expecting a child by him!" Can you imagine the sorrow of her heart? She can go to church, visit with friends, but in her heart there is this continual anguish—an internal function of the heart. Some of you may be here and regularly attending this church, and there is sorrow in your heart that this congregation knows nothing about. It's something going on inside of you and it's in there all the time.

Consider the functions of the heart in these verses:

"When they heard these things, they were cut to the heart" (Acts 5:33). Something was happening inside these angry Jews. They were convicted, cut to the heart.

"With the heart man believeth" (Romans 10:10). Believing is something that happens inside, internally.

"The word of God ... is a discerner of the thoughts and intents of the heart..." (Hebrews 4:12). Our intentions are internal.

All these verses speak of something internal happening. You can be with other people while this type of internal stuff is going on and they may have no idea because it is an internal working of the heart. Now these internal things do find expression. Even if they are covered, they will find expression eventually in some form because there is nothing in the heart 🌟 that doesn't find expression.   *Is that true?*

Out of the Heart

Now notice now how the verses in this next set refer to things that come out of the heart:

"Thou shalt love the Lord thy God with all thy heart..." (Mark 12:30). This verse is an example of something that comes out of your heart in expression toward God.

"I will praise the Lord with my whole heart" (Psalm 111: 1). This is praise coming out of the heart as an expression of the heart.

"...and that seek him with the whole heart" (Psalm 119: 2). Seeking Him is an action expressing what is in the heart.

"...out of the heart the mouth speaketh." (Luke 6:45)

"...out of the heart proceedth evil thoughts," (Luke 6:45)

"...from your heart forgive everyone his brother their trespasses" (Matthew 18:35). Forgiveness is an expression coming out of the heart.

Do you see the difference between the two categories? Internal functions happen within the heart, and expressive functions come out of the heart.

What does this say to us?

Thoughts, reasoning, meditation, feeling, pondering, etc. are all functions of the heart. Some are within and some come out. These functions of the heart are tied to some extent to the three components we discussed earlier.

In our mind, we have thoughts, reasoning, and mediations—all happening in the mind.

In our will, we purpose, have intentions, and make resolves.

In our emotions, we feel sorrow and joy, hope and despondency, fear and contentment.

Conscience

I referred to the mind, will, and emotions as

components. There is another component reflected in the Scriptures we read that I haven't said much about. It is called the conscience. In Acts 7:54 we read, "... they were cut to the heart." That reflects a function of the heart.

The conscience seems to have elements of thinking, feeling, and choosing. It doesn't fall neatly into any category. But it is part of the heart and it serves an important function.

Summary

We find, then, that the heart has specific functions. These functions reflect components with specific characteristics—the mind thinks, the will decides, the emotions feel, and the conscience convicts.

The Scripture gives directions for each of these components. We read about transforming the mind (Romans 12:2). We are told to submit our will to the will of God. Even Jesus surrendered His will to the will of His Father. "Nevertheless, not my will, but Thine be done" (Luke 22:42). We are told to "put off" some kinds of feelings—anger, wrath, jealousy, fear, etc.—and to cultivate such feelings and dispositions as joy, peace, and contentment.

Now that we have seen how the heart functions, we are ready to look further at how to care for the heart.

Chapter 2

Devotion of the Heart

When biblical writers refer to the heart, what actually do they mean?

It seems to me that Bible teachers today, wanting to answer that question, too often find a particular verse that refers to the heart, and from that verse, they form their conclusions about what the heart is. Some have concluded the heart refers the deep feelings inside you. Others say it is the will—the intents and motives that drive your choices. Still others seem to equate it with the mind—the thinking and reasoning part of your inner being.

My conclusion is that the heart involves all the

components we have been looking at. It includes our thinking. It includes our choosing. It includes our feelings, as well as our conscience. The heart is that inward, non-material part of our being.

So what is the heart for? If we think of it as the mind, it is for thinking. If we think of it as the will, it is for choosing. If we think of it as the emotions, it is for feeling. If we think of it as the conscience, it is for discerning between right and wrong. But is there a way to summarize what the heart is in an overall sense? Or is there a "heart of our heart," a center, or core part that tells us what the heart is or does in a basic or central sense?

Again, different writers and teachers will have different answers.

The heart seeks an object of devotion

If I were to try to describe one thing, or the main thing, or the overall thing the heart does, I would say the heart seeks to devote itself. If this is so, the object of the heart's devotion is the most important consideration in anyone's life. Let's explore this further.

What is the greatest commandment God gave to His people? A lawyer asked Jesus this question one day, and Jesus replied, "Thou shalt love the Lord thy God with all thy heart" (Matthew 22:37). Somehow the heart is tied very closely to this idea of loving. What we want to explore in this session is the tendency of the heart to set itself on something. My belief is that the human heart was made to set itself on God—to devote the whole life to Him, or in Jesus' words, to "love him with all our heart."

Let's break this down.

1. The human heart seeks an object of devotion.

I said the heart "sets itself on something," but what that means is that there is something the heart really, really, really wants. It's what our hopes are based on. What is that one thing your thoughts tend to come back to over and over? What is that one thing that you always have in the back of your mind directing that stream of choices you make all through the day? If you can answer those questions, you will find what your heart is set on, what your heart is devoted to.

When I say the heart seeks an object of devotion, I don't mean that only one part of the heart that is doing this. All the components of the heart are involved. This is what we think about. This is what guides our choices. This sets the tone for our emotions —for how we feel.

Now think about our world today. What are some things people set their hearts on?

I was doing some research some time ago, and I came across an article in the US News. This was back in 1988, and it was an Olympic year. As I recall, the article was entitled, "Sports Crazy." It began by saying that the United States "has truly become a sports-crazy nation." The writer quoted different authorities to prove his point. One man was a sociology professor at Penn State University, who said something like this: "For many Americans, sports has replaced traditional religion as a means of establishing basic values." I thought that was quite an insightful comment from a secular source. One thing people set their hearts on today is sports.

What else? Self, possessions, money, religion, and power—these are things people devote their hearts to every day. What is it for you? Different people set their heart on different things. For you it may be one thing, and for your friend it may be something completely different.

I believe the human heart is such that it can take virtually anything and make it an idol. The point is that the human heart seeks an object of devotion. Whatever the heart is set on will direct what the heart thinks about. We are especially sensitive to information that will help us achieve what we are devoted to. Money, sports, or sensual pleasures will direct the heart's thinking. Furthermore, our hearts are continually making choices based on what the heart is devoted to. We want to fulfill our desires and realize our hopes. Our feelings then tend to reflect how successful we are. If we get what our hearts are set on or at least if we advance toward it, we feel good. If we lose it, or if it is threatened, we feel bad.

For example, if our heart is set on money and we have a financial loss, we feel dejected and down. If we make money, we feel happy. For each one of us, the heart is set on something or someone. There is something that is most high in our hearts. Human beings are made that way.

2. The heart was made for devotion to God.

I believe our hearts were made to be devoted to God. We see this reflected in the Old Testament as well as in the New Testament. When Jesus said, "Thou shalt love the Lord thy God with all thy heart," He was quoting from Deuteronomy 6:5. The Jews called this the Shema. It was what they were to teach their children. "Hear, O Israel: The Lord our God is one Lord: And thou shalt love the Lord thy God with all thine heart, and with all thy soul, and with all thy might."

For the Christian, this means we should set our hearts on God. We are to be devoted to Him. We are to love Him. Our thinking should be centered on God, continually returning to Him. Our choices should continually come back to the commitments that we have made to Him and the love we have for Him. You cannot read the Psalms without sensing the feelings that are involved in this devotion. "O how love I thy law! it is my meditation all the day" (Psalm 119:97). The psalmist was regularly enjoying the presence of God, wanting to know Him, learning about Him and His ways and His works. Christians enjoy thinking about what God has done. It gives us joy to hear the things God is doing in someone's life. That's the heart of a person who is devoted to God.

What kinds of stories thrill you? If a ball game thrills you more than the works of God, if the stock market thrills you or dejects you more than the works of God, then something has taken over the rightful place of God. Your heart was made for devotion to God. He made us for Himself, and He wants us to set our hearts on Him.

3. The object of your heart's devotion will shape you.

Here is something I had trouble understanding for a long time: The object of your heart's devotion will shape you. Your life will move toward whatever you have set your heart upon—that object of your heart's devotion.

We can look at any of the things we listed earlier that people tend to set their heart on. Let's look at money. If money is the object of my heart's devotion, then that is what I will think about. Money will shape my choices. And when I come to the end of life, I will be characterized, more than anything else, by the money I have made. If money is my life, then my decisions, my thoughts, and my feelings will have been centered on that pursuit.

The startling thing is that whatever I set my heart on will actually shape my mind and my way of thinking. It will determine what kind of will I have—my resolves and plans and ambitions and choices and commitments. It will shape my feelings, too. I will become more and more like the object of my heart's devotion. It will make me.

where does genetics come in?

People whose heart is set on money have hearts that become calculating hearts. They're continually thinking and deciding in terms of accumulating more. That's what they think about and what gives them thrill. It's what makes them want to get up in the morning or not want to get up.

Some years ago, I was holding meetings in a community, and the pastor asked if I would be willing to do some visiting. We went to visit an elderly lady in a nursing home. Before we arrived, he told me about her husband. This man, Mr. Cope, had died a number of years before, and he had lived for money all his life. The pastor had visited him on different occasions and tried to talk to him about the Lord, but he never could get through.

One day the pastor was visiting in their home, and he needed to use the restroom. When he asked to use their restroom, the couple said he could but there was a problem. It wasn't working properly, and so right now, they said, they were using a bucket. So, the pastor used the bucket. While he was in the restroom, he began to wonder what the problem was, and so he took a quick look at the toilet. He found that the problem wasn't a big problem at all, and so he offered to fix it. He discovered that the husband had been unwilling to pay for a plumber to come fix the toilet, and they had been using that bucket for a couple of years just because he didn't want to pay to get it fixed.

Mr. Cope lived for money. Later, this man became sick and had to be taken to the hospital. He literally fought the staff when they wanted to remove his belt because it contained over $40,000 dollars. He carried some of his treasure around with him!

The pastor visited Mr. Cope when he was in the hospital. He was in bad shape. In fact, he was dying. For the first time Mr. Cope was willing to listen to the pastor talk about Jesus. The pastor shared why Jesus came and how we can be forgiven for our sins if we put our trust in Him. Mr. Cope listened, and then the pastor asked him if he would want to give his life to Christ. Mr. Cope said, "Let me think about it." That was encouraging because at least he seemed open to considering the possibility.

So the pastor arranged to come back in a few days. This time Mr. Cope was so weak he could barely speak. What do you think was on the pastor's heart? Will Mr. Cope give his heart to Jesus? But the pastor had barely arrived when Mr. Cope motioned for him to lean closer because he had something to say. As the pastor leaned in, he listened with disappointment as Mr. Cope asked him if he would buy a piece of land he had to sell. He was unable to get the man back to what really mattered. And that's how Mr. Cope died.

The heart that is set on money becomes calculating —it thinks continually in terms of gain. That's all it wants to think about. You might have played with this idol in your life and consoled yourself, "But I still go to church." Unfortunately, there are many church-goers who have money as the number one priority in their lives.

We could put other things there.

But whatever you set your heart on, as you move towards the end of life, you become more and more like it. The object of your heart's devotion shapes you.

I remember as a young married man working for a painter one winter. Sometimes when I went into the paint store, I'd meet an old man who came to the same store. I could always count on him telling a dirty joke when he was there. He was the kind of person who repulsed me. How had he become a dirty old man? It was determined by what he had set his heart on as a young man. He started to think that way as a young man, and he continued to think that way, and he became more and more like what he had set his heart on.

I remember another man whom I knew when I was about twelve years old. My family was relatively poor, so at a young age I began working at a weekly flea market in our community. I worked for a man who sold potatoes. I'd carry 50-pound sacks of potatoes to the cars of the ladies that bought them and needed help. The man would give me $5.00 for the day.

There was an Amish man who came to visit the potato vendor, and I remember the dirty stories they would tell each other. What upset me most was that here was a man who professed to be different by his appearance, but his heart was set on the same things as the man who sold potatoes who was not a Christian.

If you don't want to be a dirty old person, then don't

start down that road as a young person. We only fool ourselves if we think we can set our heart on something and not become like that. The truth is that if you set your heart on anything other than God, eventually you become disgusting. God is the only object of devotion who will redeem us, who will change us into something good.

It's always easier to look at others, but let's be willing to look at ourselves. The truth is when I was a young man watching that old man, I struggled with enjoying those same thoughts. Even as an older man, I have to guard my heart because the potential is still there. We had better be careful when we look at others with disfavor—we may easily harbor the same sin in our own hearts.

I remember when the Lord spoke to me and told me that I still didn't have complete victory over impure thoughts because I didn't really want it. God's conviction was so powerful, and I came under such conviction because I was harboring wrong desires in my heart. I didn't like the guilt of overtly thinking dirty thoughts, but neither did I want them to go too far away. So I would push them away but hope they would come back.

We can deceive our hearts this way. As the Lord says through Jeremiah, "The heart is deceitful and desperately wicked" (Jeremiah 17:9). So again, we had better be careful when we start pointing fingers at other people because we could be harboring the same sins in our own hearts.

The object of your heart's devotion is going to shape the kind of person you are. When you are making decisions and face a crossroad, what is it that tends to pull you one way or the other? What makes you say "no" to some things and "yes" to others? More than anything else, it is what you have set to your heart on, what you really, really want.

4. *The object of your heart's devotion will color all the expressions of your heart.*

Not only does what you set your heart on shape your character, it also colors all the expressions of your heart. If you set your heart on money, you will become like money. But also, the expressions of your heart—your words and actions—will be colored by the object of your heart's devotion. Your choices, your thoughts, and what you believe will be tinted by what you are devoted to.

Have you ever noticed that people who are devoted to money will believe it is okay to skip church services in a pinch? And way too often they are "pinching." Do you follow what I'm saying? What you set your heart on is going to influence all the functions of your heart —your feelings, your choices, your thoughts. There's nothing in the heart that can continually stay hidden. It will eventually come out.

As church people, we typically don't go around saying, "I'm devoted to money." The preacher might just preach on it the next Sunday. We don't want others to know these things, so we put up a nice front instead. In fact, we might be devoted to money, and give more than anyone else in the church. It's a way to protect our idol. That can happen. Whose is going to confront the biggest giver in the church? We can't fund the addition without his cooperation!

But even if we try to hide what our heart is set on, it will come out. It will color our thoughts. It will come out in our conversations. It will show up in our attitudes. It will give life to our feelings—what makes us excited and what makes us upset.

Whatever is the object of our heart's devotion is going to find expression and come out. Those who know us best will know what is important to us by our words, our actions, our attitudes, our plans, and our emotions.

When our heart's devotion is God

The beautiful part of this is that that when we set our hearts on God, He will find expression in our lives! Jesus said, "Those who pray in secret, God will reward openly" (Matthew 6:6). What is Jesus saying here? He is talking about the object of your heart's devotion. If your heart is set on God, it cannot be hidden. It will find expression. God's presence will shape you. You will become a particular kind of person. And that devotion to God will find expression in your words, your praises, your thoughts, the things you muse on, your joys and your sorrows, so that those around you will know what you are devoted to. They'll know it because it cannot be hidden.

This doesn't necessarily mean that the person who loves God will always be the first person at church. You can be the first person at church as a cover for what you did just an hour before. I'm talking about the kind of spirit you have. You cannot deny the object of your heart's devotion, especially to those who know you best—it will come out. People are going to sense it. If you are devoted to God, what comes out of your life will be a sweet, sweet savor to other believers. Do you like to be around people whose hearts are set on God? They love Him. Jesus is on their lips because He lives in their hearts. They reflect and think about the works of God—what He did for them today and how He watched over them last week. They talk about it. They tell others about it. Jesus is in their hearts.

How do we think about sin? Sometimes we talk about problems we have—the sin in our lives as well as sin in the lives of others. Even those conversations will be shaped by your devotion, your commitment. They can be shaped in good ways by our love for God. Have you ever been with a group of people who are happy, but you have sadness in your heart that rips deeply—and you cannot talk about it there? Do you know what that is like? We face those feelings at times when we are close to the heart of God because the anguish in our heart is a mirror of the anguish in the heart of God. He, too, is grieved by sin. If you have someone in your life you care about who is involved in sin, your heart had better be torn! God's heart is. I don't mean that the sorrow destroys you. Acquaintance with God during those times enables us to carry our sorrow. Paul talks about the care of the churches that he had continually on his heart. He says, "Who is grieved and I'm not grieved? Who wanders astray and it doesn't tear at my heart?" (from 2 Corinthians 2:4).

Devotion to God will come out in the expressions of our life—it will color the things that excite us, the things that thrill us. What comes out of us when we talk is a mirror of our devotion.

5. *The result of replacing God is idolatry.*
John the Apostle concludes his first letter with this appeal: "Little children, keep yourselves from idols" (1John 5:21). The result of replacing God is idolatry. If there is something in your heart other than God that

occupies your mind as the supreme thing—the thing you come back to and think about more than anything else, it has replaced God. If the decision-making issues in your life—what guides you in the things that you choose to do through the day—is someone or something other than God, He has been replaced.

It is not wrong to be a carpenter or a farmer. If you are a carpenter, many of your decisions will have to do with how to run your business, but be careful! It is so easy to be a godless carpenter or a godless farmer. To run our business without thought of God or without thought as to how our lives can contribute to the Kingdom of God is futile. Jesus said, "Seek ye first the Kingdom of God and His righteousness." If you are farmer, the burning questions should be, "How can I do this for the glory of God? What will stand out to people about me when I die? Will it be how great a farmer I was? Will it be about how I bought a dinky little farm and grew it into five farms? Or will people say that I was a person who put my life into the Kingdom of God, and did it as a farmer?" You can do that today if your heart is set on God. If our farms have replaced God, if our businesses have replaced God, if some other desire has come to occupy that place within us, then we are living in idolatry.

How can we know if we are serving idols? There are a number of tests to help us know what our hearts are set on.

1. *An idol is anything that takes the place of God as the object of the heart's adoration or worship.*

What do you honor? Whom do you honor? What kinds of people really catch your eye? If your heart is set on money, it will be people who make money. If your heart is set on building, it will be people who are superb builders. If you heart is set on God, it will be people who are close to God. What kind of people do you honor? Where is your worship, your honor, and your adoration?

2. *An idol is anything that takes the place of God as our primary reason for living.*

What is your reason for living? Do you live for God? The apostle Paul said, "For me to live is Christ" (Philippians 1:21). What's the primary reason for your living? Do you get up in the morning to please Him? Do you make plans to know Him better? Do you spend time thinking about who He is? Do thoughts of God give you energy and vitality? Does God have anything to do with what time you set your alarm for? Would you feel lost and forsaken and hopeless if you did not have God? Without God, would your life go on as normal, or would you lose your reason for living?

3. *An idol is anything that takes the place of God as the guidance for life.*

What shapes your life's goals and guides you in major decisions? What orders the direction of your life? What charts the course? What causes you to say 'yes' to some things, and 'no' to others? The proverb says, "In all thy ways acknowledge him, and he shall direct thy paths" (Proverbs 3:6). God wants to be our guide, our "shepherd," because He knows the way. He knows what is best. He has plans and purposes for us. When something or someone else takes that role, it has replaced God and become an idol. Is money your shepherd? Is pleasure your shepherd? Is sports your shepherd? Whoever is your shepherd will guide you into certain places and certain activities. The Good

Shepherd wants to take you to His pastures and lead you to His water.

4. An idol is anything that takes the place of God as the primary reason for sacrifice.

What do you sacrifice, and what do you sacrifice for? We all sacrifice. It's not a question of whether we sacrifice or not, but what we sacrifice for what. We don't sacrifice lambs and heifers anymore as they did in the Old Testament, but we do sacrifice. We give up time. We give up sleep. We give up energy for certain things. Do you get tired sometimes for the Kingdom of God? Do you lose sleep or do without in order to bless people around you? What do you sacrifice for?

If I were to ask you if you think that God should be the object of our heart's devotion, you would probably give me an instant "yes." But the real question is "Where are your altars?" What have you given for what in the last month? Do you find yourself regularly sacrificing for things earthly or for things heavenly? We're only fooling ourselves if we think God is our supreme love and then we sacrifice more for something other than God.

Are you just fooling yourself? What do you really worship? What is your heart really set on? Idolatry is primarily a heart issue. It's having something or someone in our hearts at the place where God ought to be. It is not wrong to get up early to milk your cows, but that had better not be the only reason you sacrifice time and energy and sleep. You might ask yourself, "What is my greater reason for milking cows? How can I experience God in my farming? Am I milking these cows for the glory of God? How can my farm contribute to the kingdom of God?"

I believe that when the heart is set on anything other than God, eventually it self-destructs. The heart actually deteriorates and you will actually lose the ability to make right choices. There are people who know that alcohol is destroying their lives, but they can't quit. They know that buying lottery tickets is destroying their bank accounts, but they can't quit. Why? The object of their heart's devotion has destroyed their will. The Scriptures speaks of people, for example, who have "eyes full of adultery and that cannot cease from sin" (2 Peter 2:14). This is saying that if your heart is set on something other than God, you will eventually lose your ability to choose otherwise. The Bible calls it bondage.

There are men who are so wrapped up in business that it is destroying their family, but they can't seem to let go of their business. There are men who are so wrapped up in sports—hunting, fishing, or spectator sports—that it is damaging their marriage, but they can't seem to quit. There are ladies and men who are so involved in ministry—doing good things for others —that they are neglecting their own children, but their identity and security comes from their ministry, and they won't give it up. They won't get it back in its proper place.

Idols aren't good for us. It is God Who sets us free and enables the heart to function the way it was intended to function. A person who loves God with all his heart and who believes what God has said will have a good heart that functions right. He will think right, choose right, and feel right. His heart will be functioning properly, the way God intended.

What is your heart set on? Someday the object of your heart's devotion will be laid bare. It troubles me that there are times I can sense that my heart has slipped from devotion to God, my love for Him has become cool, and I'm still expending the energy. That was the problem at Laodicea. They thought that they were rich and increased with goods but in reality in God's sight they were poor, blind, miserable, and naked. God is pursuing your heart. Open your heart to Him. He wants to show you if there are areas you have been giving your heart to other than to Him. God is a jealous God, and He wants your heart.

We live in a culture that is not geared to making a godly person. If you are going to be a man of God or a woman of God, you will have to consciously set your heart on God. You will need to be prepared to go against the flow of those around you, even some Christians. It is so easy to think that we look good, and in reality our hearts are slipping away from devotion to God. I say this kindly.

God knows where your heart is. And I pray you will have the courage and wisdom to devote your heart to Him.

Recommended reading:
Seeking Him (for ladies)
Lord I want to Know You (for ladies)
A Man after God's Own Heart
The Pursuit of God
Knowledge of the Holy

Chapter 3

The Effects of Sin

We looked first at how the heart functions and then at the need to devote our hearts to God. We are now going to take a look at how sin affects our hearts. This is not an easy subject—the effect of sin on our hearts is not something we enjoy talking about.

What happens to the human heart when we sin?

We want to look at what God has to say about sin and our hearts. What would Jesus say about sin and how it affects human beings? I wish I could give you a glimpse into the lives of people I have known who have disregarded God. Obviously I can't do that, but I am grateful that the Scriptures don't just give us commands, but stories. And some of those stories show us what happens when people sin.

There are many Scriptures we could start with. Genesis tells us the sad story of how sin entered into the world and how that sin affected the heart of Adam and Eve—how it ate away at the character of their descendants until we read in Genesis 6:5 that "God was grieved in His heart because the imaginations and the thoughts of their hearts were evil continually" (Genesis 6:5). Men's hearts were filled with evil continually as a result of original sin.

In Ephesians 4 Paul describes the effects of sin on the heart. He writes, "This I say therefore, and testify in the Lord, that ye henceforth walk not as other Gentiles walk, in the vanity of their mind, having the understanding darkened, being alienated from the life of God through the ignorance that is in them, because of the blindness of their heart: Who being past feeling have given themselves over unto lasciviousness, to work all uncleanness with greediness" (vv.17-19). Lasciviousness is a word we don't use very often today, but it refers to sensual desires. Uncleanness is another form of sexual sin. The NIV says, "They have given themselves over to sensuality so as to indulge in every kind of impurity, with a continual lust for more."

The next verse is refreshing: "But ye have not so learned Christ."

We're going to go back, however, and look at verses 17 through 19 and notice some of the effects of sin and how damaging it is to those components of the heart that we studied earlier. Again, I'm using the word "components" to describe different areas of our hearts, such as the thinking of the mind, the choosing of the will, the feeling of the emotions, and the judgments of the conscience.

The questions we want to consider include: How does sin affect the mind? How does it affect our will? How does it affect our feelings and our conscience? I want to explore what the Scripture says about these questions. Paul describes these people as "being alienated from the life of God." That's a significant description. God never intended for the heart to function right when it's not set on Him, when it doesn't know Him. The heart just won't work right— you will not think right, you will not choose right, and you will not feel right. Your sense of right and wrong will be messed up. It will become twisted if you don't know God. "Being alienated from the life of God"— that is the saddest part of this whole description.

Think about tractors as an example. If you were to try to run your diesel tractor on gasoline, what would happen? What if you were to try to run it on water? What if you decided that diesel fuel is getting too expensive, so you mix it with water? Would your tractor work? If it was designed to run on diesel, then you'd better put diesel in it! You will ruin your tractor if you do not use it as it was designed to be used. If our hearts were designed to be devoted to God, we'd better devote them to God. If you are devoted to something else, you are going to ruin your heart. Sin is damaging to these components of the heart. Let's look at these components of the heart individually.

The Effects of Sin on the Mind

Paul says that those who are alienated from the life of God live in "the vanity of their mind." This means there is futility and emptiness in their way of thinking. He also describes them as "having their understanding darkened." The understanding is in the mind. Their understanding is darkened.

What happens when you try to walk in the dark—especially if you try to walk in unfamiliar places in the dark? You run into things, bump things, and make mistakes because you can't see right. What if we just start dimming the light? Now, as long as you're in familiar territory doing familiar things, you can possibly get by. Eventually, however, we need light.

When the mind is cut off from God, the lights go out. It is a serious problem to be separated from the light of God in a world of sin. When the understanding becomes darkened, we stop thinking right. We enter into sin and begin to walk in our own ways. Because we are cut off from God, we begin to confuse good and evil.

Isaiah 5 is a powerful passage that starts out talking about a vineyard. God likened Israel to a vineyard He had planted. He "planted" them and fenced them in and intended that they would produce grapes, but instead He got wild grapes. This is not what He was looking for. And God begins in Verse 8 to pronounce a series of woes. "Woe unto them that that join house to house, that lay field to field." In Verse 11, He says, "Woe unto them that pursue strong drink." And then in Verse 20, He proclaims, "Woe unto them that call good evil and evil good; that put darkness for light, and light for darkness; that put bitter for sweet and sweet for bitter!"

When our hearts are alienated from God through sin, we can no longer think straight. Pardon my bluntness here, but we do things that are downright stupid! We can no longer make clear decisions about right and wrong, and we begin to make moral judgments from a totally wrong perspective. We confuse good and evil.

My brother-in-law was a pilot for many years. He doesn't fly for a living now, but at one time he was a bush pilot in northern Canada. He told me that high altitude flying is always dangerous for pilots of small planes. Their cabins are not pressurized, and they run short of oxygen. They get to altitudes that are so low in oxygen that although they are breathing, they are not getting the oxygen their bodies need.

The most dangerous part is that they think they are doing fine! If they have radio contact, they begin to make statements that don't make sense. The person on the ground will begin to pick up on the problem and ask, "Are you flying too high?" The pilot will say, "No, I'm fine." Then he says something else that doesn't make sense. The person on the ground will advise the pilot to fly lower, but he says he's doing great. Many times, that is the last they hear from him. The pilot thinks he is thinking straight, but in reality he is confused.

When you are cut off from God, your mind doesn't work right. You are not thinking straight. Your understanding is darkened. You will begin to confuse good and evil and embrace harmful ideas as though they are helpful. You absorb ideas into your thinking that are not true.

In Romans 1 we have a description of how sin affects our thinking. Verse 21 says, "Because that, when they knew God [notice the departure begins here], they glorified him not as God; but became vain in their imaginations, and their foolish heart was darkened." When we no longer retain God in our thinking, when we are no longer in fellowship with Him, when our heart is not devoted to Him, we begin to think stupid things. We will think that good things are bad for us, and we will think that harmful things are actually for our health and redemption. It goes on to say, "Professing themselves to be wise, they became fools."

When we observe these things happening to actual people—to people we know and interact with—we see and feel the tragedy. It is incredibly tragic. Do you know what it's like to watch somebody who thinks he is doing right and actually he is destroying his life? That's what we're talking about here. They think, "Oh, I'm fine." In reality, they are headed for destruction.

I remember sitting with a man some years ago. He was married, but he and his wife were separated at that time. He had another lady that he liked, and he was spending time with her. He told me he didn't understand why his wife would get so upset when he brought this other lady home. Yes, he said, he knew he was committing adultery, but in his judgment the love in their marriage was over and so he wondered what was the big deal? I was sitting there wondering how a man can think like this! How can he think that having another lady in his life and bringing her into his home should not affect his wife? When we are alienated from the life of God, we think stupid things. We embrace false ideas. We begin to live by those ideas. And it takes us towards destruction.

The Effects of Sin on the Will

How does sin affect the will? Our thoughts and our choices are closely related. When we think wrongly, we choose wrongly. Again, people often think they're thinking very well. In fact, they believe their thinking and their choices are far better than those of people who want to do what God says. In their ignorance, they call obedience legalism. They talk about the grace of God as though it enables them to sin freely.

The Bible says, "The grace of God that bringeth salvation hath appeared unto all men, teaching us that, denying ungodliness and worldly lusts, we should live soberly and righteously and godly in this present world" (Titus 2:11, 12). What does the grace of God do? When you experience the true grace of God, it will teach you to say "no" to sin. That's what it will do. If you can't say no to sin, you don't have enough grace from God. It isn't that you get more grace so you can sin more, but that you get more grace so you sin less. That is the effect of the grace of God—it teaches you to say "no" to sin. The sad irony of it is that sometimes people think they are thinking better, when in reality they are thinking worse.

How does sin affect the will? People who sin think they are now in charge of their decisions. They have the illusion that they are more free. But sin will never let you stay in charge. Sin will eventually take control of you. That is the effect of sin on the will. It enslaves the will. In our passage in Ephesians 4, it says, "who being past feeling have given themselves over to lasciviousness." They haven't taken control; they have lost control. They have not become free; they have yielded their freedom and become slaves of sin. The terrible irony is that they think they are now free to do whatever they want to do, but in reality they are giving themselves over to sin and are becoming enslaved. They don't realize it.

When I was a boy, I attended a children's class in which I was chosen to be part of an object lesson. The teacher had a spool of thread that she wrapped around me and told me to break. I broke it. She wrapped it around me several times and told me again to break it. You know what she did next, don't you? She wrapped and wrapped and wrapped. You can take a thread and if you wrap it often enough, you can tie up the strongest man on earth so that he cannot break it.

That's how sin is. It will eventually be you master. Sin never intends to let you be in charge. You say yes to sin often enough, and eventually you won't be able to say no to that sin.

We're talking about the bondage of the will.

Notice that the bondage of the will, like the darkening of the mind, is the result of being cut off from God. It is in relationship with God that the will is actually free. We are enabled by God to choose the things that are best for us.

Now again, although I've spoken of the mind and will separately, there's a good bit of overlap in their actual functions. The mind and the will interact closely. The mind receives information. If I reject the truth of God and embrace my own ideas or the ideas of sin, with that wrong information I begin to want what is ruinous to me. I actually desire the things that destroy me. I don't think, at that time, that they are destroying me, but I actually seek after the very things that will ruin me. And I don't want the things that would bring redemption to me and give me freedom from this sin. When you see this happening in the lives of people you know, it is tragic.

I remember a young man I went to school with. We

weren't the closest of friends, but I remember him coming over to my house one day and I went out to see him. He pulled in, rolled down his window, said hello, and then said he'll be on his way again. Then he explained to me what he was doing. He said he had told his father he was going over to see John. His dad was okay with that, so he had come to see me. Now he was ready to go do the things he really wanted to do.

I remember listening to this same young man getting angry at a teacher and using unprintable language. A couple of months after we graduated from high school, we were shocked to hear that this young man had run away from home. I didn't know where he had gone, but later I learned that he had gone to a place in Texas that helped people with drug addiction. In his "freedom" to do as he pleased, he had come to the place he could no longer do what he wanted. He got scared because he realized he was in bondage.

I've talked to people who have come to realize that what they're doing is ruining them. It is destroying their lives. In anguish, they say, "I can't quit!" What has happened? Their will is enslaved. They thought they were making their own choices, but in reality their choices are now being made for them. Sin has taken over.

That's what sin does to the heart. It makes you a slave. It will turn you into its servant. You will do its bidding and you cannot get out. Even knowledge doesn't help when sin is in charge. Paul says in Romans 7, "The things I know I should do, I don't do! The things I don't want to do are the things I find myself doing!" In verse 24 he exclaims, "Who can deliver me from the body of this death?" Who can give freedom from sin?

Paul goes on to say, "I thank God through Jesus Christ our Lord" (v. 25). No sin is too strong for Jesus Christ! He can break the power of sin. But people too often refuse to turn to Jesus because they've gotten a taste of doing as they please, and they don't want to give that up. They keep thinking, If I just try a little harder, I can get rid of this sin, and I can still be in charge. Of course, it won't work! Deliverance comes only through Jesus Christ.

Several years ago I knew a young man who was a senior in high school and was tired of the strictness of his parents. He wanted to do things they didn't want him to do. He wanted to be involved in the sports programs, dances, and other school functions. He began to live a double life, and he purposed that he was going to break ties with his family and his church and live the way he wanted to live after he graduated from high school.

Meanwhile he conformed outwardly, but secretly pursued a life of sin. His church had revival meetings that fall, and this young man along with two other young men in his community covenanted together that they would not yield in the invitation to Christ. Through those meetings, those young men sat in stony silence. But on the last night of the meetings, there was much prayer, and the Spirit spoke strongly to this young man. He broke down, went to the evangelist, and asked for help to invite Jesus into his life.

The evangelist and the young man went into a private room to pray. This young man could not pray. He tried to pray, but no words came, and his face began to twist and contort as he struggled to call on God. The preacher came out of the prayer room and asked the congregation to pray for them as this spiritual battle raged! As the young man continued to call out to God, he was delivered.

He became a powerful man of God, one of my closest friends. I thoroughly enjoyed being with him. A number of years ago he died on the streets of New York City in a subway station while passing out tracts. In him, the power of sin was broken by the power of Christ.

What that young man did not realize was that when you take hold of sin, sin takes hold of you. It takes you into bondage. Sin makes you a slave. There is no man or woman here tonight that is big enough to master sin. We simply cannot handle it. That is a reality. I can't change that reality; all I can do is describe it for you. That is the effect of sin on the will.

I remember another young man who came to a Bible School where I was teaching. We had prayer and Bible study every day. One day he came to me and confessed that he could not break the cycle of filthy thoughts in his mind. He had watched sensuous movies and had fed his mind on pornography. He said, "Every time I try to study the Bible, all I can see is those pictures and movies!"

Sin will bind you. It will take your will captive, so that you no longer are in charge of your life. No sin is a safe sin. It is ruinous to the mind and will.

The Effects of Sin on the Emotions

Let's talk about the emotions now. How does sin affect our feelings and emotions? In the previous session I looked at emotions briefly. So before we get into how sin affects our emotions, I would like to explore the functions of the emotions in a little more detail.

1. *Emotions are motivators.*

Our feelings urge us to do things. They tend to push and pull us around—motivate us to respond to circumstances and people. I talk to a man recently who said he does not have feelings. He had some sort of physiological problem that made him emotionally flat. He said he does not get excited or depressed—he just doesn't feel anything. I wondered how this man could function. He's a godly man. When it's time to eat, he eats. When it's time to read his Bible, he reads his Bible. When it time to go to work, he goes to work. But no feelings. I thought, How do you exist? God intended for us to feel. Feelings motivate us.

There are times when feelings so flood us that we will do things that seem incredible. When we are very frightened, for example, that fear can motivate us to do things that later we have no idea how we could run that fast or jump that high or lift that amount of weight!

A number of years ago I came upon the scene of an accident where the bishop of our church had pulled out in front of someone driving at an excessive speed. Roman (the name of the bishop) was driving a Volkswagen. He had been hit just behind the front fender on the driver's side, and the body of his Volkswagen from the front tire diagonally across the vehicle was gone. The engine (located in the rear of the car) was strewn all over the road. Roman was lying with his legs still in the vehicle, and his body draped down on the pavement. He had a puncture wound in his head and was unconscious. I had no idea what to do.

Suddenly I heard a scream. I looked over at the other vehicle, which was a full-sized convertible, lying upside down in the lawn beside the road. A number of other people were with me and we rushed over to the upside-down car. We saw legs sticking out from under the car thrashing about, and we heard someone yelling, "Let go of my head!" Without thinking, we grabbed the side of that full-sized car and lifted it up on its side. I remember thinking how light the car seemed. I've often wondered since then—if we would get the same few men around the same car could repeat what we did that day? We were feeling fear, the adrenalin was pumping, and we were powerfully motivated to do something.

2. *Feelings are reflectors.*

We go through experiences in life and emotionally we feel what we're going through. Sometimes we wish we wouldn't because we have not only pleasant feelings, but uncomfortable feelings as well. God created us this way.

When our feelings are reflecting our circumstances, we don't necessarily choose our emotions. You don't go through part of a day and suddenly think, "Hey, I haven't laughed today yet. I think it's time to have a good laugh."

I'm not saying we don't have any control, but that the feelings we have in any given circumstance are less voluntary—they simply reflect what we are going through.

How does sin affect our emotions?

Do you know that our emotions reflect the ruin of the soul? When people sin, their lives become a mess. They get into binds and difficulties as a result of their sin, and then they want out. Sometimes they want out of the consequences without changing their life of sin

—they just don't want to feel bad. But I have sat with people who have experienced the ruin of their souls and the ruin of their relationships. Do you know what happens? When they try to describe what they are feeling, the tears begin to flow down their cheeks. I wonder how many times I've seen that happen. It happens to believers and unbelievers. When we engage in sin, it will ruin us, and we pay a high emotional price tag.

I remember calling my neighbor one morning. He had a dump truck, and I needed some gravel. His wife answered the phone and I asked, "Is Don there?" Don was not a saved man, but I was taken by surprise when Wendy, his wife, said flatly, "He didn't come home last night."

I wasn't sure what to say. I knew Don did some drinking, but I didn't know it was that bad. I stuttered around a bit and said I would try to get in touch with him later. The next day my wife was in town and she met Wendy in a store. She went up to Wendy and asked how she was doing. Wendy burst in to tears, turned around, and walked away.

Wendy was an unbeliever. She didn't have God to go to, and she didn't know what to do with the sorrows in her heart. Emotions reflect the ruin of the soul, the ruin of relationships, the ruin of things gone wrong.

When the heart is cut off from God, the mind is cut off from God, the will is cut off from God, and the emotions are cut off from God too. When we are cut off from God, He is not there to comfort us in sorrow and to encourage us in our weakness.

The most common emotional effects of sin are fear and guilt. Think about the first sin. When Adam and Eve disobeyed God, they heard the voice of God in the garden, and what does the Bible say? They were afraid. That is the first reference in the Scripture to an emotion. Adam and Eve were afraid, and they hid.

Sin will increase your fears. You may not recognize it immediately, but sin will increase your fears. It will also cause guilt. We feel guilty about sin. Because of fear and guilt, it becomes the goal of the sinner to feel good. He is tired of feeling bad. The unfortunate thing is that in order to feel good while not wanting to face their sin, people sin more. What happens? It becomes a vicious cycle.

Before the sinner understands what is actually happening, he gets angry at anything or anyone that stands in his way of feeling good. If you warn the sinner not to do something, he reacts, "Who made you my preacher? Why are you telling me what to do?"

Often sin gives immediate thrills and eventual heartache. The sinner will seek those thrills to feel good because he can't stand facing the reality and misery of his guilt. He hates not feeling good, so he thinks he must do something.

Again, the bigger issue here is that sinners are cut off from the life of God. It is that sad reality that results in emotional misery.

The First Thrill

Recently I attended a retreat where I heard a talk on addictions, and I learned something. They said typically with addictions the first thrill is the greatest. After that, the thrill tapers off, so the addict is continually coming back seeking to experience that first thrill again.

For the believer, for the child of God, the thrill of the presence of God moves in the opposite direction—it increases. David wrote, "At thy right hand there are pleasures [not just for a moment but] forever more!" It is not just a first thrill—it is forever!

The experience of a decreasing thrill with sin corresponds to the description in Ephesians 4. Paul describes sinners as "being past feeling." Sensuous pleasure-seeking results in a dulling of the feelings. This results in frustration for an addict. And sometimes the sinner is touchy and irritable because he lives in a state of continual frustration. It is the result of wanting to feel pleasure while experiencing a diminishing sense of thrill.

Pleasure, of course, is not necessarily wrong. God intended for us to enjoy things. But when you make pleasure your highest pursuit in life, instead of allowing pleasure to be a product of seeking to do what is right, you begin to pursue pleasure for itself. You begin to measure right and wrong by what brings pleasure or what denies pleasure. And soon you are willing to do wrong to find pleasure. The effects of sin are always counterproductive. Instead of leaving us full and satisfied, sin leaves us empty and frustrated.

This is what Paul is talking about in Eph 4. When a person lives in sin, his life becomes a quest. He is seeking for something. And when a "hungry" person turns to sin to satisfy his hunger, he becomes hungrier. He increases that yearning. Life becomes a quest for something that will give him peace and happiness, and that searching of a sin-ruined soul is endless. He never finds it. He finds momentarily thrill, and then sorrows are back again, greater than ever. The momentary pleasure of today is drowned out by the multiplied sorrows of tomorrow. There are people who spend their whole paycheck in one evening, and they get pleasure for that evening, but the rest of the week they live in misery for what they have squandered. "The way of the transgressor is hard!"

The Effects of Sin on the Conscience

Let's look now at the conscience. This is the part of our heart that distinguishes between right and wrong. I don't understand everything about the conscience, but I have benefited from a book written by O'Hallesby on the conscience. It is out of print now, but it is a book I'd recommend.

The effect of sin on the conscience is to scar it. When the conscience is cut off from God and no longer close to God, our moral awareness becomes self-centered rather than God-centered. What actually determines right and wrong? From the Bible we learn that morality is rooted in the character of God. Whatever is in accord with God is right, and whatever is not in accord with God is morally wrong. Read the book of Leviticus starting around Chapter 18 and you will find God saying, "Thou shalt do this, I am the Lord," and "Thou shalt not do that, I am the Lord." Basically what He's saying is, "This is in accord with who I Am. That is not."

Contrast that with the sinner who has taken charge of his own life and is making his own decisions. His moral awareness is centered on himself. His subconscious model is, "Whatever is in accord with me and my will is right. If it's against my will, it's wrong. If it makes me feel good, it's right, and if it doesn't, it's wrong." Do you see how subjective that gets and how twisted from the true standard of what is actually right and wrong? A sinner who takes charge of his own life and does what he wants in spite of what God says will often be an irritable person because he can't make reality revolve around him. Because life doesn't work out the way he wants, he is unhappy.

The conscience also acts as a judge. It is a blessing that God made us with a conscience. I am amazed at how people can violate their conscience, boldly sin, and yet their conscience refuses to just roll over and die. God will still talk to them through their conscience. Sometimes right in the middle of their sin, their conscience will rise up and say, "You are a miserable sinner!" Isn't that wonderful? I'm grateful God made us that way. The conscience is incredibly tenacious and resolute. It hangs on and refuses to back down in spite of being violated. It will continue to act as a judge and often make the sinner tremendously miserable. His own conscience will tell him, "You are rebelling!" or, "You are cheating!" He has to live with that and so he either seeks more pleasure or eventually he comes to his senses and says, "I give up. I can't really run my life."

On the down side, however, the conscience will also act as a judge of others. Sin damages man's conscience both ways whether he's thinking of himself or thinking of others. He will condemn some people when they are not worthy of condemnation, and he will commend other people who are not worthy of commendation. Sometimes, in his own life he will commend himself when he ought to be scolded and at times he will scold himself when he ought to be commended. Sin damages those functions of the conscience.

I have referred to sins of the flesh, such as drunkenness and immorality. But such things as pride, envy, and self-righteousness are also sinful. Although they are not as visible, they too are damaging to the heart. When I think I have made myself good in God's sight, and I think that I can merit the grace of God, I begin to measure spirituality superficially. In self-righteousness, my mind enters a subtle darkness—I don't see God or people or things correctly. My will takes on chains of bondage—I become enslaved to making myself look good. My feelings are driven by wrong values, and I live in unhealthy fear of people and their opinions rather than a healthy fear of God. My conscience judges myself and others on false premises—on whether we measure up to my standards of righteousness.

All sin is damaging to the heart of man. We need the daily cleansing of the blood of Jesus and the sanctifying work of His Holy Spirit to purge us of sin so we can think right, choose, right, feel right, and make right moral judgments.

Chapter 4

The Effects of Being Sinned Against

In the last session, we considered the effects of sin on the heart. We were looking at personal sin. In this session, we are going to look at another dimension of sin. We want to consider the effect of being sinned against. How are our hearts affected when people sin against us?

I begin with a passage in Matthew 18 where the disciples ask Jesus a question. "At the same time came the disciples unto Jesus, saying, Who is the greatest in the kingdom of heaven? And Jesus called a little child unto him, and set him in the midst of them, and said, Verily I say unto you, except ye be converted and become as little children, ye shall not enter into the kingdom of heaven. Whosoever therefore shall humble himself as this little child, the same is greatest in the kingdom of heaven. And whoso shall receive one such little child in my name receiveth me. But whoso shall offend one of these little ones which believe in me, it were better for him that a millstone were hanged about his neck, and that he were drowned in the depth of the sea. Woe unto the world because of offences! For it must needs be that offences come; but woe to that man by whom the offence cometh!" (Matthew 18:1-7).

When Jesus uses a term "offense" here, He's talking about doing things against others that potentially cause them to stumble. He especially warns against offending little ones. But notice that He says, "It must needs be that offences come." What does He mean?

In Luke 17:1 Jesus is again speaking about offenses: "Then said he unto the disciples, It is impossible but that offences will come: but woe unto him, through whom they come!" The NIV captures the sense of the word "offence" by saying, "Things that cause people to sin are bound to come." Jesus goes on to say as He did in the passage from Matthew, "It were better for him that a millstone were hanged about his neck, and he cast in to the sea, than that he should offend one of these little ones. Take heed to yourselves: If thy brother trespass against thee, rebuke him; and if he repent; forgive him. If he trespass against thee seven times in a day, and seven times in a day turn again to thee, saying, I repent; thou shalt forgive him. And the apostles said unto the Lord, Increase our faith."

How we think about suffering

Our culture lives under the continual quest for a sorrow-free life. We like to safeguard ourselves against getting hurt, against experiencing trouble of virtually any kind—interpersonal trouble, calamities, losses, and so on. And unfortunately, watered-down Christianity sometimes presents this same unrealistic "peace and happiness" type of thinking. You become a Christian and you will be happy. It becomes a Christianized version of the same illusion. You come to Christ, and your troubles will be over.

Now I do believe that following God brings incredible pleasure. But I also believe that in this world, following God brings suffering. Jesus did not promise that we will be delivered from all sorrow just by following Him. Some of the most incredible, soul-thrilling experiences in my life have been because of my relationship with God. God can thrill us in ways that can defy all description and break all the bounds of our ability to contain it. But my walk with God has also brought me into the most difficult experiences I have ever faced.

There were times in Jesus' ministry when He exclaimed, "Father, I thank You!" Other times, however, He was in agony. If we believe that coming to Christ will make our lives sorrow-free, we believe an illusion. The "health and wealth" gospel (I don't even like to call it a gospel) is popular among some people today, but I want to tell you that it's not the Gospel of Jesus Christ! His Gospel is rich with blessings, but it is also tear-stained with struggles.

We need a Christianity that anticipates suffering and offers God's grace for that suffering. That is the kind of Gospel we need. It was with suffering, trials, and difficulties that the Apostle Paul came to understand and to hear from God, "My grace is sufficient for you."(2 Corinthians 12:9) There will be times when you ask God to change or remove something from your life and God says, "I'm teaching you a different lesson this time."

It seems to me that the first lesson God teaches new Christians is that He can remove anything from their lives. That makes us excited! We have a problem in our lives, we cry out to God, and He removes it. Our response is, "God is wonderful!" God really does remove painful things from our lives. But it seems that eventually He says, "Now, there's another lesson you need to learn—I am still God when you hurt, and when you keep hurting, and when nothing seems to change. I am still who I am. I am still God!"

That's what Paul learned in 2 Corinthians 12. God told Paul He would not remove the thorn, but that His grace would be enough for him. I'm not at the place the Apostle Paul was—I have not yet started getting joyful when I see trouble coming. I'm just not there. But Paul said, "I rejoice when I see infirmities, troubles, and difficulties because I know that the power of Christ is going to be made known" (2 Corinthians 12:9, 10).

There will be offences.

Let's come back to Jesus' words in Luke. He said, "It is impossible but that offences will come." That is the kind of world we live in—a world of sin. Even though we may not be personally engaging in sin, though we may be resisting sin in our own lives, we still live in a world of sin. As a result of that, we are going to experience trouble and difficulty. We live in a world where sin abounds. And people will sin against us.

If you grew up in a home where your father and mother loved each other and they loved God, you have an incredible blessing. You have been sheltered from thousands of sorrows that others live with every day. Sin brings sorrow. As I talk about sin and sorrow I wonder—wherever you are reading this—think about the sorrow in the last 24 hours that happened within a five mile radius of you. Did tears flow down people's faces? For some people, was it sorrow beyond tears? Were hearts numbed by sorrow?

Some years ago when I began to become convicted that we were not reaching out to people in the community around us, some of us began to try to do so. And people began to open their lives to us. I remember one man who wanted help for his marriage. After I talked with him, he wondered if I would talk to his neighbors. He said they have marriage problems, that sometimes from his house he could hear them arguing in their house. I asked if they wanted to talk to me, and he said he would find out. They did want to talk, so I went to visit them. These people were in the middle of horrendous conflict! I talked with them, and then they told me that about four blocks down the street, they had some friends who were having marriage problems too. They asked if I would be willing to talk to them. I began to think, Is this the most God-forsaken place in the world? Does everyone in town have marriage problems?

The truth is that these kinds of struggles are all around us. We live in a world where people sin against each other. Unfortunately, we are sometimes so involved in our own world that we are blind to the sorrows of people around us.

Those of us who have grown up in Christian homes where father and mother loved each other too often do not realize how protected and shielded we have been. I have taught many classes at a winter Bible School. One year I was teaching a class entitled "Helping the Hurting." I gave the students the assignment to write out an experience where they had been hurt and to describe how they struggled as a result of it. A number of students sweated over the assignment and finally came to me and said they just didn't know what to write. These young people had had a good home, a good church, and loyal friends and had never been hurt significantly. They couldn't think of anything to write about. I thought, My, oh my! You have been so sheltered! But just wait—with the kind of world we live in, your sorrow will come eventually.

According to Jesus, there will be offenses. Somewhere along the way, it's going to hurt. You are going to face things that are too big for you. That's how life is. If you've grown up without experiencing a lot of hurt, thank God for it. Don't go around looking for trouble. Instead, rejoice that you have been spared and sheltered! The reality is, however, that sometime you will suffer. That is the kind of world we live in.

And so, although everyone experiences suffering and sorrow, not everyone experiences it in the same measure. It doesn't always come out equally. That's one of the things that can increase our struggle—we start comparing our sorrow with the sorrow of other people. We start looking to see if our load is as big as theirs. We see that someone else's children are all at home, happy, growing up, and following the Lord. Their crops are doing well every year, and they seem to have it so good.

I am presently reading through the book of Job, and I find that he and his friends both wrestled with this question—who ever heard of any one person experiencing this much sorrow? So, on top of his losses, Job experienced the misunderstanding of his friends. They kept begging Job to repent because they thought that the only reason a person would go through this much suffering would be as punishment for sin! They kept saying, "Repent! Recognize what you've done wrong!" Imagine how all this felt to Job! Finally toward the end of his speeches he cried out, "If somebody would just hear me!"

Did you ever feel that way? "If someone would just understand...."

Sorrow doesn't come to us in equal measure. Sometimes people become embittered because what they are going through seems like so much more than what others are going through. It seems so senseless.

We sometimes make generalizations like, "You give to God and God will give to you." Or, "If you respect others, they'll respect you." Or "If you invest time in your children, they will follow God." These generalizations are often true, but then sometimes I think God allows us to experience the opposite. We give to God and He allows something to be taken away from us. Or, we do well, and we experience trouble.

In this life, sorrow does not always follow sin exactly. There are people who sin regularly and openly, and yet they seem to be getting along fine. It doesn't seem like they have as many sorrows as Christians who are doing their best to live right. The reality is that sorrow does not always immediately come upon everyone who sins.

Being sinned against can result in stumbling.
When people sin against us, we easily stumble. Children are especially vulnerable. In Matthew 18:6 Jesus says, "Whoso shall offend one of these little ones which believe in me...."

The subject of offending children is controversial, I know. And I am going to try to be balanced. My belief is that children are being sinned against in our culture and that as Christians we should not assume that once they meet Jesus, they won't have any struggles as a result of being sinned against. Jesus will give them a premise for working through their struggles, but being sinned against as a child is a serious thing. Jesus warned against offending little ones.

Children are especially formative. That is a reality. You can do things to children that you cannot do to adults. They are exceptionally impressionable. In children, offenses can obscure the face of God. Notice Jesus warns us lest we "cause these little ones which believe in me to stumble." Little ones who believe in Jesus can turn away from Him because others have sinned against them. There are people who grow up in an environment that develops in them an aversion for church. They say to themselves, "If this is what Christianity is, then I don't want anything to do with it. If he is a Christian, I don't want anything to do with Christ."

I remember working with a single lady who said she becomes nauseated when she sees a very godly man. That is a very unfortunate association. When she was growing up, her father gave the appearance of godliness—he stood behind the pulpit and portrayed godly character in his sermons. At the same time, he was using his daughter for his sensual pleasure. She developed an aversion to godliness.

Can you hear what is being said here? Little ones can stumble as a result of being introduced to adult sin. "These little ones who believe in Me...." Offenses can obscure the face of God. These little ones develop resistance toward God, not because of who God is, but because somebody stood in their way of finding God. This is one of the effects of being sinned against. This is one way a person's sin can affect the hearts of other people. The result of such offenses is anger, bitterness, and resentment deep in the soul.

The response to the offense determines the ongoing effect on the heart.

It is not just what happens to a person that does the shaping. The response of the offended person has an even greater effect on the heart. People experience things in Christian homes that should not happen. Likewise things happen in church that should never happen. But they do. These offenses themselves can be hurtful and devastating. But much of the lingering effect has to do with how the offended person responds. So we have two things to consider: 1) The offense. 2) The response. Surprisingly, it is the response, even more than the offense, that determines the ongoing effect of being sinned against.

Someone has said life is 10% what happens to you and 90% how you respond to it. In view of what weight Jesus gave to offenses, that's probably light on the side of "what happens to you." But I'd certainly agree that how we respond to the offense will have much to do with how that offense will affect us long-term.

Anger is a common response when we are offended.

We get hurt by somebody, and our normal response is to get angry. When we internalize the anger, we develop a bitter heart. Notice in the example I gave of the father who was sinning against his daughter—she was a very angry person, but her anger was all internalized. Her friends and acquaintances did not experience her as an angry person, although there were tensions at times. Even she was not aware of all the anger she had internalized. Anger is a normal response to being hurt, and we need to be understanding of people who are angry. At the same time, internalized anger is dangerous. People who grow up in an environment where it is unacceptable to acknowledge anger often have no idea how angry they are until they honesty begin to face the situations in their lives where they have become angry.

Some people teach that if you have been hurt by someone during your childhood, you need to go back and relive that experience and feel what you felt back then in order to be healed. My belief is that this approach is overplayed. I think this reflects an influence of psychology that is unhealthy. At the same time, I believe if you have people and experiences in your past that you are still angry about, you will never get deliverance from them until you face them honestly. I think you have to look at them. I also believe that by refusing to look honestly at difficult experiences, people avoid acknowledging that they are angry.

In Ephesians 4:26 we read, "Be ye angry, and sin not." This verse is confusing to some people. Why does it say, "Be ye angry," and then a few verses later it says, "Put off anger"? I don't have a full answer, but I do understand this: when we are angry, it is easy to sin. And so, immediately after saying "Be ye angry," Paul warns, "Sin not." Maybe he is simply recognizing that sometimes we will be angry. The NIV translates it with that idea, "In your anger, do not sin." I'm not a Greek scholar, so I don't know which is the better translation, but I think sometimes we will be angry. And Paul warns us to be careful because when we get angry, it is easy to sin.

Paul goes on to say, "Let not the sun go down upon your wrath." If you keep anger until the next day, it is even more dangerous. You keep it for a week or a month—there are people who are still angry about things that happened ten or twenty years ago—that anger is exceptionally dangerous. It is ruinous to the heart.

As you read this, take a few minutes to pause and ask yourself if you are angry, resentful, or bitter. This is our tendency as human beings. We hold on to anger in our hearts. Paul warned not to let that happen—don't hold on to your anger even overnight! It will change forms.

I've talked to people who are resentful about something that happened years ago, and they will say, "I'm not angry." But if you stick around for awhile, you will hear resentment coming out, especially when certain topics come up. They talk about "what he did" and "how often he did" and "where he did it." These resentful comments tend to leak out without the person realizing it. He will say he has forgiven, but the resentment is still there.

When anger turns into resentment and bitterness, it is kind of like bad breath. Everybody else knows it, but you! People around you know it—they can sense it. You may think you are not angry because it feels different than your initial anger, but anger can change forms. Resentment is just a different form of anger. And if there is resentment in your heart, it will come out.

Internalized Anger

In Hebrews 12:15 the writer warns us that we should not let any root of bitterness spring up and trouble us. Bitterness defiles many people. Notice the progression here. Anger kept in the heart will turn into resentment and bitterness. This grows like a root and springs up in trouble. You will stop growing spiritually. Bitterness will damage your heart and keep you from drawing near to God. And then it will turn into interpersonal sin. It will put walls between you and other people. You will hold grudges, harbor bad attitudes, and try to avoid certain people. Notice again that the way we respond to difficulty is shaping us even more than the difficulty itself.

Bitterness in the heart causes us to interact internally with people. This is familiar to all of us— we can become very proficient at carrying on arguments in our hearts. Someone says something nasty about me and I carry that conversation around in my heart. I argue with that person over and over for a week even though he doesn't know anything about it. I carry that person around with me in my mind. And when I argue with him, I always win. I set him straight. I rehearse all the things I should have said when I talked to him. I go over it and over it. By the time I go over the argument twenty times, I am excellent at arguing. And I am also very miserable. If I internalize that anger and keep it alive in my thoughts and feelings, it damages my heart. You can't draw near to God with internalized anger.

Suppressed Anger

Some people hold their anger inside and try valiantly not to think about it. Their anger simmers under the surface like a boiling kettle with the lid jammed on tightly. They not only try to keep this inner turmoil hidden from everyone, but they try not to acknowledge it even to themselves. They are very angry, but if you meet them on Sunday morning, they look like they have just been redeemed. They don't show it on their face because they have suppressed their anger—they try to live as though nothing hurtful happened.

To use another analogy, suppressed anger is like throwing all our junk in a closet in the back of our heart. When we are around people, we close the door tightly. But as the "stuff" accumulates, it becomes more and more difficult to keep everything in that closet. The doors sometimes pop open, and the smelly junk falls out. It takes a great amount of emotional energy to keep those doors closed when we are interacting with others—we fear letting anyone know all the turmoil we have deep inside. If you suppress your anger like that, eventually you are going to be depressed.

In 1Kings 19 we have the sad story of Elijah getting depressed. Now with this story, there are no doubt factors other than anger bearing on his emotional condition, but Elijah does seem to have become resentful. Listen to the way he talks, and you will hear it in his speech. He thought things were unfair. He tells the Lord, "I have been very jealous for the Lord God of hosts: for the children of Israel have forsaken thy covenant, thrown down thine altars, and slain thy prophets with the sword; and I, even I only, am left; and they seek my life, to take it away" (v.10). Essentially, Elijah is saying, "It's not fair!" If you live with thoughts and feelings and attitudes of "unfair," you are destroying your heart. That is a reality. If that is the internal climate of your soul, eventually you will get depressed. It takes a huge amount of emotional energy to be angry, and eventually you run out and go down.

Proverbs 15:13 says, "A merry heart maketh a cheerful countenance: but by sorrow of the heart the spirit is broken." When we harbor resentful thoughts in our hearts, we eventually are carrying a load we cannot bear. Imagine your heart is like a kettle. When other people are around you make sure all the anger is stuffed into the kettle and the lid is on tightly. You smile, you are friendly, and you seem like a nice person. All the time you are living out of the part of your heart "above the lid." When you are alone, you let your thoughts muck around in the tangled mess in the kettle, but then someone comes by, and you slam the lid on the kettle again and relate to them "above the lid." That kind of living will drain you. It takes tremendous energy to continue relating this way and eventually it takes you down.

So we are seeing that it is how you respond to the difficult situations and people in your life and what you do with your anger that determines the ongoing effects on your life.

Now, in our culture, being sinned against has become the means of escaping responsibility for sinful behavior. There are people who will say things like, "The reason I have problems is because of my dad, my mom, my preacher, etc." And so, for many people the reason for looking into the past is to find out why they are angry. And when they have figured out who caused their problems, that is where they stop.

What is God's way?

God recognizes that people sin against each other. And He holds the offender accountable for his actions. At the same time, God holds me responsible for my responses. I am not responsible for what my father did or didn't do in my life, but I am responsible if I become resentful toward him. I am responsible if I refuse to go home, if I put up walls, and if I write him off.

When I was in Europe last fall, I met a lady who struggled with a lot of hurts. She had grown up in a non-Christian home and she said, "I was at the place where I felt that if I never saw my sister again, it was okay." She is now a believer. I was teaching on anger and on the need to take responsibility for how we respond to those who have hurt us, and she said, "This stuff is heavy! I don't know what to do with it!" But she eventually came to the point where she knew the anger she was carrying was destroying her. Putting up walls was protecting her from more hurts from her sister, but it was at the same time allowing resentment to do its destructive work inside of her.

If I am comfortable with walls built by resentment in my relationships, then I have a problem God wants me to deal with. You may be thinking, "That isn't fair. That puts the entire burden on me!" But actually it puts on you only the burden of your response—and that is what gives you hope! Consider this: If your spiritual condition depended on those around you—specifically, those who hurt you—where would you be?

What hope would you have for growth and change? The reality is that God holds us responsible for our behavior because that is the way we can grow and mature through the events of our lives.

God will take care of the offender. I need to learn that in order to forgive. If someone hurts me, I have to remember what Jesus says about that person. He does not let him off. He says it would be better if a millstone would be tied about his neck and he would be drowned in the bottom of the sea then to cause others to stumble. God will take care of the offender. I don't need to worry about the offender. My job is to pay attention to how I'm responding and to the choices I am making in my own heart.

My belief is that we can experience freedom and growth when we are willing to trust God and forgive those who offend us. When you have been hurt and your heart is filled with resentment and anger and God puts His finger on your heart and shows you that you are not at peace with someone—your father, your in-laws, a brother in the church—God is holding you responsible for how you respond. If you allow that resentment to stay in your heart, it will ruin you and keep you from spiritual growth.

How do we get deliverance?

Later I will talk about repentance and heart change and how to clean the junk out of the heart, but here let me mention a couple of basic principles we must understand if we want to find freedom from resentment that has accumulated in our hearts.

1. Trust God

You will not forgive people in your life until you

[handwritten margin notes: Really? Isn't this ha-ha, God'll get em?]

realize you have been focusing on the wrong place. As long as you're looking at the offender in your life, you will have trouble forgiving.

As a Christian, I looked at people who had done things against me, and I couldn't get over the fact that they were wrong. Some of the people even came and confessed to me that they had done wrong, and I would think about those things and think how awful they were. In fact, where God really broke me was in a relationship I had with a preacher. Did you know that preachers can be carnal, too? I would think about something he had done and how wrong it was! I knew I needed to forgive. So I would forgive him, but ten minutes later I would have him right back in front of me and be thinking again, "That was so wrong!" Now the deceptive part of this is that resentment is often based on truth—what the person did was wrong! That is, of course, the reason we have to forgive. We do not forgive things that are not wrong.

Do you know what that is like to let something go (in your heart) and then bring him right back and go round and round reliving what he did and accusing him?

What finally brought deliverance to me was realizing that as long as my focus was on the person, I could not forgive. Until you take your eyes off the person who has hurt you and refocus your eyes onto God, there will be no deliverance. God is the answer to our problems. The problem with resentment is that we have a wrong focus. We have a resentful view of what someone has done to us instead of a trusting view of who God is and what He can do for us.

What does it mean to trust God?

2. God can turn bad into good

How do we get our eyes on God? We start by believing God is over our lives. Nothing we experience is outside of His full awareness and His sovereign rule. This doesn't mean He is causing others to do what they do, but that He is present in every situation and He is at work to bring about His good purposes.

Here is our trust: God is big enough to take things that come at us as destructive and turn them into things that build us. When I came to understand that truth, I had a premise for no longer focusing on what others were doing, but on my responses before God. In that trust, I had a foundation from which I could forgive my offenders. You can get freedom from resentment and bitterness when you turn your eyes to God and trust Him.

The confusing part, of course, is that we don't see God's purposes immediately. All we know is that it hurts! All we see is that it's damaging. It has not yet produced its fruit and we don't see how it can. We think, "It's the worst thing that could have happened to me!" Sometimes the things that are the most painful in our lives come when we are at our lowest and we think we can't take any more. In those exact times, we need to come back to God, get our eyes back on Him, and trust.

God is a redeemer. He is an incredible redeemer. He can take anything in our lives and cause the effect to be good. That is beyond our understanding! I understood that God redeems sinners, but I had no idea that God could redeem everything about me. You may not agree, but I'm asking you to consider the redemptive power of God.

I believe that God can even redeem our sinful past.

There are experiences in my past that if I had my way, I'd take a scissors, cut them out, pitch them in the trash can, and never look at them again. I'm ashamed about some of those things, wounded by others, regretful about many things I have said and done. But God redeems everything.

If you question what I am saying, think about the apostle Paul. What was he like before he met Jesus? In his own words, he was a murderer, a blasphemer, and a persecutor. He was "injurious," which means he hurt people. But he said, "God set me forth as an example of His grace." Near the end of his life, he wrote a letter to Timothy and talked about who he was before He met Jesus. It wasn't like he cut out that part of his life and put it in some divine trash can. I am supposing that in his travels he met people who were wicked sinners and he told them about salvation in Jesus. I can imagine some of them saying, "You don't know the kind of person I am. You don't know what I've been into." And Paul was likely polite enough not to smile, but in his heart he probably was thinking, "Go ahead and tell me." As people shared their stories, he could tell them, "I know what it's like to be ashamed of the past! I was like that too!" That part of his life that was "trash" became a treasured testimony when God redeemed it. That is the grace and power of our incredible God!

So, when people sin against us and we focus on who did what and when and where and how often and for what reasons, our eyes are not on our Redeemer. God wants us to believe that whatever has come to us from anybody, by His grace He can anoint, and by His power He can redeem.

Some of the most beautiful people in the Bible as

well as some of the most beautiful people I have ever met are those who have been sinned against—deeply and repeatedly. What happened? They trusted God and the grace of God turned the devastation into deep and rich character.

You may be thinking, "Yeah, that's for them, but the things I'm going through… I don't see how God can do that." Trust Him. If somebody is hurting you, it's not wrong for you to feel pain, but be careful! Don't stay there. Bring it to God. You can believe that anything coming at you hurtfully, by the grace of God can be turned into righteousness in your heart, into something good, into the substance of soul that will make you a beautiful person in God's sight.

It is in this context of trusting God that we can forgive. Once I learned that I could trust God in this way, I could release the people in my life who were hurting me. As I kept my eyes on God, I found that I did not continue to bring up the offenders in my mind's eye to accuse them. My hands were open—I had no compulsion to grab them and pull them back again.

I don't know what is in your life, but God does. He knows what you have gone through this past week. He knows what you have gone through this past year. He knows the people and the situations that are troubling you and offending you. I urge you not to let your offenders destroy your heart. It won't actually be your offenders that destroy you as much as your responses to them.

The human heart is precious. The writer of the Proverbs said, "Keep your heart with all diligence" (Proverbs 4:23). Keep your heart because it is the source of all your living. If you truly want to protect your heart, keep it free from sin because sin will ruin it. If you want to protect your heart, you will need to learn right responses to offenders.

Searching the Heart

We've been talking about the heart. We have recognized how the heart functions. We have identified different parts of the heart: the mind (what we think), the will (what we choose and purpose), and the emotions (what we feel). We also talked about the conscience, which acts as a moral guide. It convicts us when we do wrong and blesses us when we do right. We've talked about sin and the effects of sin on the heart. We have recognized the effects of sin on the mind, the will, the emotions, and the conscience. We have also looked at how being sinned against affects the heart, and we concluded that it is not only what people do to us that affects us, but even more how we respond to what others do.

Looking at the heart this intently, you may sometimes feel like you are being turned in-side-out. That will continue as we consider now the subject of "Searching the Heart." God can do exactly that—He intends to turn us in-side-out.

God's Role in Searching the Heart

Through the prophet Jeremiah, God had this to say about the human heart: "The heart is deceitful above all things, and desperately wicked" (17:9). Let's think about the word "deceitful." I don't know Hebrew, but I am told that this word "deceitful" has the same root as the name "Jacob." The name Jacob literally means "one who grabs the heel from behind." His name means a trickster, a deceiver—someone you definitely can't trust. You never know how he's going to take you. Jacob lived up to his name for many years. He had taken his brother's heel during birth, and he continued to perfect his tactics in the years that followed.

God says the human heart is a "Jacob"—it trips us up. It deceives us, takes advantage of our weaknesses, and causes us to fall.

And then God asks a question: "Who can know it?" We don't easily understand what is in our hearts exactly because they are deceitful and wicked. So how can we "know it"? How can we understand what is in our hearts? The Lord answers that question in verse 10. "I the Lord search the heart, I try the reins...." The word "reins" is an older expression that we don't use as much, but it refers to the mind. The verse continues, "...even to give every man according to his ways, and according to the fruit of his doings."

Clearly, the Scriptures teach us that God is the expert at searching what is in our hearts. His work is to search out and find what is hidden in the heart of man. Have you given God the freedom to search your heart? The answer to the question, "Who can know it?" is God. God says, "I know." He knows your heart like no one else, including yourself. He knows everything about the human heart.

1. *Only God truly knows the heart*

When I speak in a public setting, I can look into people's eyes, and I can read things in their faces that reflect what is in their heart. Much of the time, we show what is in our heart by the expression on our face. I can sometimes see people in sorrow, and sometimes as I preach I can see that my words are bringing comfort to those sorrowing hearts. At other times, I can read conviction of heart on people's faces. Sometimes I can tell that a person has a question. But I can't read hearts perfectly. We learn sometimes it is not safe to let people know what is in our hearts. We learn to "blank" our expression and hide what we are thinking or feeling in our heart because we don't want people to know what is there.

But the Lord knows. He is never baffled by a blank expression on our face or deceived if we try to appear one way when we feel quite different on the inside. The Lord knows our hearts.

2. *Trying to know my heart apart from God is delusion*

I will be deluded if I think I can know my heart apart from the help of God. Learning to know our hearts—who we are and what is motivating us—is a tough job. Sometimes we think we know what is in our hearts—we think, for example, we are being kind or thoughtful. And later we realize we were actually quite selfish in our motivation. At other times we have things in our heart we want someone else to know about. If we are experiencing sorrow, for example, we typically want to share it so somebody else knows what we're going through.

Ironically, we can sometimes catch others in self-delusion quicker than we can see our own delusion. We might hear a person say, for example, that he is sad or hurting. But we have been interacting with that person for some time, and we think, "Yeah right! You don't know yourself! You are nothing but bitter. You want sympathy. It's sticking out all over you!" Do you ever think you know what is really in another person's heart better than that person himself?

As I look at my own heart and as I make these observations about others, I have come to realize how difficult it is to be honest about my heart. My belief is that it is impossible to really know our hearts apart from the help of God. He is the One—the only One—who knows us, and He can reveal our hearts to us.

3. *God wants us to invite Him to search our hearts*
Psalm 139 starts out saying that God knows everything about us. He knows when we sit down and when we get up. He knows when I recline on the Lazy Boy, when I feel like getting up, and when I don't. He knows if you are a night owl or an early bird. He knows if you are sorrowful or bitter. He knows everything about us! And the Psalmist goes on to say that no matter where I go, I can't get away from God. I

can go down into the sea, I can go up in the air, I can go out into a desert or anywhere I choose, but God is there and He knows me. He knows all my thoughts and what's going on inside me.

In light of that omniscience, the psalmist cries out, "Such knowledge is too wonderful for me—I can't understand that kind of knowledge!" He goes on to describe that even when we were formed in our mother's womb, God was there, putting us together. He knit our tissue. This One who knows everything created us. He knows all about us.

And then at the close of the psalm, the psalmist prays, "Search me, O God, and know my heart. Try me and know my thoughts, and see if there is any wicked way in me."

May I ask you—do you give God that kind of freedom? Does He have the freedom to search your heart? I understand the Hebrew word translated "search" is a very strong word. It is a word that could be translated "ransack." The psalmist is asking God to search him in-side-out!

When I was a boy, we had a drawer in our home we called the "junk drawer." I don't know if you have such a thing in your house, but we did. When we could not find something, we would often check the junk drawer. We would pull it open and sort through it. Typically, the junk drawer was a mess and once in a while we gave it the help it needed. When we couldn't find something and we were pretty certain it was in there, we would sometimes pull the entire drawer out and dump all the contents on the table. Then we would sort through all the "stuff" that had accumulated. And we would find things in there that were not fit even for a junk drawer. We would gather the trash and put it where it belonged. And we would organize the rest of the stuff and put it back in again. Then we knew what was in the junk drawer.

"Search me, O God, and know my heart... and see if there be any wicked way in me." Are there things in your heart that are not fit to be there? Does God have the freedom to dump it all out, go through it, show you what is in your heart, and take out what doesn't belong? Have you ever given Him that kind of freedom? That's a little scary, isn't it? What is in your heart?

God's methods can also feel scary to us. If you were a drawer, how would it feel to you to be pulled out and have all the contents of your heart dumped out on the table? The psalmist says, "Try me and know my heart." Have you ever noticed that we tend to think we are not truly ourselves when we're under trial? That's how we say it, isn't it? "This is not how I normally act." But when God wants to show us what is really in our hearts, He usually does so by taking us through trials. There we learn to know who we really are.

I was counseling a man a number of years ago who was a car dealer. He found out I needed a vehicle. One day he called and told me he had found a car at an auction. He asked, "Can you come and check it out?" So I went with him and we took it for a test drive. I drove the car, and it seemed fine to me. Then the dealer said, "Let me drive it." Now, he knew how to test-drive a vehicle—I mean he put it to the test! He tested the acceleration, braking, and steering—he wanted to know not only if it would drive fine under normal conditions but also how it would do under stress. That is how you know the real condition of the vehicle. That makes sense, doesn't it?

Now, suppose you were testing the brakes of a vehicle. When you press lightly, they work fine. But when you brake a little harder, the car starts to shake. Did you ever drive a vehicle when the rotors are slightly warped—you know how the vehicle starts to chatter when you try to brake? Now, the car might say, "Just go easy and I'll do fine. Most of the time I don't shake. It's just when you brake too hard that I have a problem." Would you say those brakes are okay? Would you judge the brakes by how they are doing when everything is going well or by how they are doing when put to the test?

But when God does that to us, we say, "That's not really me." We start shaking when God puts us under stress, and we label it as a bad day. We declare, "I'm not normally like this!"

"Search me, try me, and know my thoughts, and see if there be any wicked way in me." I ask you again, does God have freedom to test you?

It is the impurities in our hearts that give us problems. The reason we invite God to search us is so the things in our lives that cause the "shaking" can be taken out. We invite Him to do that because those are things that will cause trouble in our personal life and in our interactions and relationships with others. God wants us to invite Him and give Him freedom to do this.

4. *God invites us to pour out our hearts*

In the last session we talked about our experiences in life and how we go through interpersonal struggles where people hurt us. We can become resentful or angry about those experiences because we don't know how to handle them. Then we put that lid on those parts of our hearts, and our hearts become an accumulation of turmoil, resentment, and bad attitudes. God invites us to pour out our hearts. This is one way to give God freedom to search us.

In Psalm 62:8 we read, "Trust in him at all times; ye people, pour out your heart before him: God is a refuge for us." God doesn't want us to fill up with care, sorrows, anxieties, and troubles. He wants us to keep a heart that is clean and open before Him. He doesn't want us to have these back areas or secret closets that no one can see. He wants us to have open hearts. He knows that when we open our hearts to Him, He can cleanse our hearts and free us from the things that will cause stress and difficulties.

5. God mercifully gives opportunities to see our hearts

In His mercy, God gives us opportunities to see our hearts even when we are unwilling. There may be times when we're going through tough experiences in our lives and we haven't recently invited God to search us and try us. We are content just where we are. God may allow trials in our lives that cause stress. Attitudes start coming out and we begin to see the kind of people we really are, without having asked specifically for His searching.

God's intent here is not to shame us or make us feel bad. He is providing opportunities for us to see what is in our hearts.

Sometimes when God begins to show me the contents of my heart, I have been ashamed and embarrassed. I remember a time in congregational life when I was interacting with another brother in the church and I came to realize that I had a rival attitude in my heart towards him. It was embarrassing because I thought I was a fairly mature member in the church. But I had a wrong attitude. So, I asked God to search me and show me what was in my heart, to show me what I was actually thinking and feeling toward this brother. When I was honest and actually wrote it down on paper, I was embarrassed to look at it! But that was exactly what was in there.

We don't gain anything by pretending it's not there, by covering it over and acting nice and pious. Opening it up may be terribly embarrassing. I decided, in that situation, that I needed to talk to the church about it —we were facing an ordination, and I thought they should know what was in my heart. So I shared it with them. I confessed my rival spirit—that I had carnality in my heart and needed cleansing. The problem was not with the other person; it was pride and selfishness in my own heart. I don't know when I wept in front of the church like I did that time. It broke my heart realizing how wrong I was and how detrimental that kind of heart is to true brotherhood.

I remember another time God searched my heart in painful ways. A single lady was living with us for a time, and she occupied a room in our basement. I like to spend time with God early in the morning, but one morning I got up a little later than normal. I dressed and walked out to the living room where I normally had my devotional time. As I was walking toward the sofa, I heard the lady coming up the stairs. We had an open stairway that came up into the living room. My immediate thought was that I needed to open my Bible or kneel down and be praying when she saw me. She came up and went into the bathroom ... and I sat there all pious and holy.

Then I met God. You open your Bible and you meet God. The Lord put His finger on my heart; He just opened it up and said, "John, you are a proud man, and you want people to think you are holy and righteous." I was smitten and so embarrassed. I began to wonder what was really driving me. Do I really seek God, or am I trying to build some kind of image?

God gives us these opportunities at times to see ourselves when we're not even asking for it. The question at that point is, "Will I be honest with God?" Will I ask God to search me even though I'm embarrassed at the things He shows me? Will I let Him search my heart and invite Him to show me what is there?

His intent is not to embarrass us, but to purge us. He wants to save us. He knows if we have pride or rivalry in our hearts, those inner sins will hinder us and hurt others. He knows we will experience problems and difficulties in relationships if we don't deal with these attitudes. They will come out in words and actions that cause conflict. They will bring trouble and sorrow both to us personally and to others. So, God is not there to embarrass us but to purge us because He is committed to our good. He gives us the opportunities to see ourselves.

6. *God doesn't force us to acknowledge the true contents of our hearts.*

Not always have I been as open as I have described here. Sometimes God has shown me impurities in my heart, and I just buttoned up my straight-cut coat and imagined, "I'm a good person. After all, I do seminars, God!"

God doesn't force us. If we would rather live with

the delusions or pride in our hearts, He will not force us. We must be willing.

On the other hand, when we are set on resisting God, He may respond in a number of ways. He may in mercy give more opportunities, or He may eventually let us have our own way. From some angles, that is a terrible truth, one that I don't fully understand. Pharaoh hardened his heart against God, but then we also have that awful record that God hardened Pharaoh's heart. Apparently, there comes a point where God may actually give us over to our own ways and even help us in our stubbornness. God is amazingly merciful, but mercy is not the only face of God.

"I the Lord search the heart..." (Jeremiah 17:10). No counselor in the world can take the role of God in searching the heart. If a counselor does not lead you to the light of God and to opening your heart to Him, but instead tries to tell you on his own what is in your heart, he may only increase your delusions. If a pastor doesn't lead you to God, then you may also experience delusion. God is the One who knows the heart better than anyone else.

The Role of Scripture in Searching the Heart

God speaks to us by His Spirit in our hearts. He also uses the Scriptures both to search our hearts and to speak to us. In Hebrews 4:12 we read, "For the word of God is quick [alive], and powerful, and sharper than any two-edged sword, piercing even to the dividing asunder of soul and spirit, and of the joints and marrow, and is a discerner of the thoughts and intents of the heart." The writer uses figurative language to help us see that God can make fine-line distinctions and exercise accurate discernment.

1. The Word of God expresses the heart of God

When we want to know how God thinks or what are His judgments on an issue, whether right or wrong, we go to the Word of God. Good "heart maintenance" calls for regular reading of the Word. In the Bible we learn to know what is important to God, what He likes, what He detests, how He feels toward people, how He responds, and what His purposes are for us. He reveals His heart to us in His Word.

2. The Word of God has a powerful effect on the heart of man

If I tell you something, you can say, "Well, that's your opinion." But if I read to you from God's Word, it's not merely my idea. It is the Word of God.

I find it difficult to properly describe the power of the Word of God on the heart of man. When a minister preaches his own ideas, people may agree or disagree. But when he preaches the Word of God, it does things beyond even the minister's awareness and expectations. It speaks with power to the heart of man because it accurately describes the condition of the heart. God's Word will do that—it will resonate deep in the heart. This is true whether God's Word is spoken or read.

If you are a child of God, and you are not regularly taking in His Word, I would urge you to start. We have such ready access to the Bible that some people seem to neglect it for its very accessibility. It has become common—not because it is too much read but because it is too easily laid aside. Some people would rather ignore the Word and go by the inner impressions they experience when they are alone. The Word, however, is what stands. People have suffered tremendously and have died to have the Word of God—just to hold it in their hands.

A number of years ago, I listened to man who grew up in an Asian country where he didn't have access to the Word in his language until he was an adult. He had never seen a copy of the Bible. Wycliffe translators had made arrangements to translate the New Testament in his dialect. This man received a copy and for the first time in his life, he read through the Gospels. He was so excited to learn about this Jesus! He read about His life, His teaching, and the miracles He performed. As he continued reading, the story was building ... and then he came to the crucifixion. He could not believe what happened. "They crucified Him!" As he read through the crucifixion, he became angry. He said, "The Man for whom I had so much hope... He died! All that power, and He let them kill Him!" He was so upset that He took his copy of the New Testament, threw it in the bushes by a river, and stomped away. As he walked away, he was mulling this over and was wondering why the story ended that way. He had been so excited to learn that this was the Son of God, and the great message to mankind. After a while he cooled down. He was still thinking about Jesus, and he realized he had not finished the story. So he went back and picked up the story where he had left off. Then he read about the Resurrection! It upended the defeat of the cross. This man gave his life to Jesus Christ. I heard him say that it was simply reading the story of Jesus Christ that changed his life!

God's Word is powerful and it speaks.

But it speaks only if we read it. You may have been a Christian for ten, twenty, or thirty years and have never read through the Word of God. I would urge you to begin. We have something precious here. You can read through the Bible in a year by reading just 15-20 minutes a day. I was challenged to read through the Bible as a young man. I had a chart to follow that told me what to read each day. Since then I believe I have probably read through the Bible every year at least once. There is a perspective you get when you read through the Bible that you don't get by reading a chapter here and a chapter there.

I remember talking about this in my own home. I was a pastor by then, and I remember my wife commenting that she didn't know if she had ever read through the entire Bible. She had a desire to, so I bought her a One Year Bible. A One Year Bible is nice because it is all laid out for you. As she read it, she would say, "This is wonderful!" Watching her joy gave me joy as well. She would come show me a passage and say, "I never knew this was in there!"

Our son was a new believer at about this same time, and so I gave him one as well. He was about 12 years old. He too read through the Bible that year.

I also remember a young lady who was struggling with assurance of salvation. She said, "I go to church and they talk about all the things I have to do, and the ministers fuss at me about this and about that." When she opened her heart, we learned that she was afraid she was going to hell. My wife and I talked to her and encouraged her to continue to seek God and not give up. About a year later, we saw her again and asked her how she was doing. She said, "I found God!" She began to tell us how one day she had begun to read Isaiah, and she said, "God is in Isaiah! I just love the book of Isaiah!" And she began to share with us how meaningful this had become to her. I was incredibly blessed! Here was this young lady who had been struggling with knowing how to pray and wondering if she was going to make it spiritually. If I would have tried to lead her some place in the Bible to help her find God, I would not have pointed her to Isaiah! I would have chosen something easier, perhaps in the New Testament.

My point is that God speaks through His Word.

When God speaks, it calls for a response. As He describes our hearts, as He shows us our motivations, He urges us to respond.

When God showed me the rivalry and pride in my heart, He wanted not only cleansing from those sins, but a change of heart. The first thing He called for was repentance—He wanted sorrow for my sin, and He then called me to turn around. He wanted to replace those sins with love and humility.

One of the things I did was to ask God to show me verses about honoring and preferring others, verses about humility and serving others. I searched the Word of God and wrote down the verses that spoke to these issues. I made a list and began reading over those verses on a daily basis. In fact, I carried them around with me and read them several times a day. I read them over and over. Then God began to show me how to live out love and humility—how to show love to those around me. Exposure to the Word of God on specific issues is life changing. It does good things in our hearts. It changes the way we think and act.

The Role of Fellow Believers in Searching the Heart

What is the role of fellow believers in searching the heart? In 1 Cornithians 14 Paul speaks about prophecy—where one person is giving the Word of God to the people of God. In verse 24 he says, "If all prophesy, and there come in one that believeth not, or one unlearned, he is convinced of all, he is judged of all: And thus are the secrets of his heart made manifest; and so falling down on his face he will worship God, and report that God is in you of a truth." Here God is speaking His words through a believer, and these words have a powerful effect on the hearers.

1. Believers have the sobering responsibility of speaking God's Word

As believers, we have this sobering responsibility of speaking God's Word to each other. Prophecy is defined earlier in the chapter where Paul says, "He that prophesieth speaketh unto men to edification, and exhortation, and comfort." Prophecy is when I speak the words of God and they edify or build up other people. Prophecy happens when I exhort others; that is, when I speak the words of God that urge them on in a right way or point them from the wrong way back to the right way. Prophecy also happens when I speak words of God that comfort those in sorrow or distress. God's Word is powerful in its ability to build up, to urge people on, and to comfort their hearts.

One time when I preached the Word of God, a man came to me afterward and shared with me how during my message God had convicted him about his music, and he needed to make some changes. I said to him, "But I didn't talk about music." He replied, "I know, but God did." I was thinking, Isn't that something? God will take His Word and say things to people that I'm not even saying as a speaker. I had no idea that the secrets of this man's heart included issues about the kind of music he was listening to. But through the Word of God, the secrets of his heart were laid bare, made manifest, made known to him. Paul says that in such situations, those who are convicted will fall down on their faces and worship God.

Prophecy will bring the words of God into the lives of others, and that work is a sobering responsibility.

2. *Believers can enable others to pour out their hearts to God*

Even as God urges people to pour out their hearts to Him, believers can also urge others to pour out to God. There are times when someone may come to you and tell you they are struggling with something—maybe their relationship with their mother-in-law or wife, or maybe a situation that seems unfair. You can know immediately that you cannot fix that problem. But maybe you can be an agent in pointing them to the One who can.

Having pure hearts and right lives provides a platform for us to urge and help others as we talk and ask each other hard questions. At times, people come to me struggling. I begin to ask them questions. I can't change what is in their life; I cannot always see what is in their heart. As they talk I begin to see some things and I ask questions such as, "Are you struggling with resentment, lust, or pride?" I can ask those questions and urge them to open their heart further and pour it out to the Lord. Once they see what is in there, they can take it to God and ask Him for cleansing and change.

And so I ask you again, does God have freedom to search your heart? How interested are you in holiness? Are you so interested in having a pure heart that you will say to God, "Even if you have to try me and put me under stress to show me what is in my heart, that's okay?"

I too am human, and I am limited. I don't know what is in your heart, but God does. Today I'm urging you to invite the Lord to search you and let Him show you what is in your heart even though it may be embarrassing. I would rather be embarrassed here than on Judgment Day. God does know our hearts, and someday our hearts will be revealed. I pray that your heart will be a heart that is purged and pure, and that the work of grace in you will bring glory to God.

Cleansing the Heart

To know Jesus and to be under His new covenant is an incredible privilege! One of the terms of this new covenant is that God will do a work in the heart. And God will do His work in our hearts wherever we are—we do not need to go to Jerusalem. We don't have to offer a certain animal or come on a particular day of the week. All over the world, God is seeking for those who will worship Him in spirit and in truth. According to Jesus, "The Father seeketh such to worship Him" (John 4:23).

We have been talking about the heart. We considered sin and the effects of sin on the mind—how people begin to think stupid things in the moral darkness of sin. We also looked at the fact that we often choose to sin voluntarily, but eventually we cannot choose because sin has taken control of our lives. And we noted that sinners live with the misery of their choices and sin's consequences.

In this session, we will look at a brighter subject. There is cleansing! We are going to explore what the Scriptures say about cleansing the heart.

As we do so, I want to bring into focus the central theme of these sessions—the call to have a heart for God, that in our inner being we are people who seek God, long for Him, and have entered a lifelong pursuit of Him. I know that we often come to God because we are in trouble and we want out. I also know that God has much more in store for us than forgiving our sins. He wants to enter into relationship with us. He wants to bring us into His eternal family. To experience that will take more than just wanting to be out of trouble.

But often the first step is taken because of the desperate circumstances we have gotten into or the miserable guilt feelings that come from living in sin. Ironically, the human heart wants to be in charge, wants to make its own decisions, wants even the freedom to choose sin; but then, it can't live with the misery of selfishness and sin.

Note how many times in Psalm 51 David cries out to God for a clean heart. "Wash me! Cleanse me! Create a clean heart in me!" This is a continual prayer in this Psalm. We don't realize how dirty sin is until we actually begin to seek cleansing. While we are enjoying sin, we don't understand what it is doing to us. It is somewhat like children playing in the mud. They don't realize how dirty they are until it's time to scrub.

As one author put it, only when we seek cleansing does the sinfulness of our heart really hit us. He said the heart that is seeking cleansing is "scorched" by its sinfulness. In many ways then, cleansing is eye-opening for us. We suddenly realize how filthy and defiled we are.

So now, let's think about how the heart is cleansed from sin.

The heart is cleansed through confession

"If we confess our sins, he is faithful and just to forgive us our sins, and to cleanse us from all unrighteousness" (1John 1:9). John shows us clearly that the way to cleansing is through confession.

But now, notice the previous verse. "If we say that we have no sin, we deceive ourselves, and the truth is not in us." From this we must conclude that cleansing is not an experience for only a select few. This is not just for people who "really get into sin." We are all in sin and we all need cleansing. Not a one of us is without sin. Every heart is defiled.

So, how is the heart cleansed? John calls us to confess our sins. And he assures us that when we confess, God is faithful—He will forgive us and cleanse us from all unrighteousness. Thank God for cleansing! Many times it is difficult for us, in our sinfulness, to see our sin. We are so used to the dirt that we don't think of ourselves as being dirty. Cleansing starts with confession.

1.   Confession means we have to face our sin

If we're going to confess our sins, we need to face them. That's a tough thing for human beings to do. We don't like to face our sin. We tend to look at the cause of our sin instead. We like to name the people who "made us" do wrong.

I have five boys who are excellent at confessing sin —that is, confessing each other's sins. If one of my boys does something wrong and I go to him and ask, "What did you do?" he will tell me what his brother did!

We see that from the beginning of sin. When God asked Adam, "What hast thou done?" Adam said, "The woman—she gave it to me." He confessed her sin. It's easy to confess someone else's sin. If we want cleansing, we're going to have to face our sin. We must look at what we have done.

When one of my boys is guilty and confesses his brothers' sins, I let him say what he wants to about the others, but then I come back and ask, "But what did you do?" "Well, he…" and off he goes again to say what the other one did. Finally, when I say it often enough, he will confess, "Well, I hit him."

We like to divert the attention away from us, to dodge away from honest acknowledgment of sin. It's hard for us to face our sins and look squarely at what we did. We not only talk about what others did, but we also talk about the circumstances. "Well, it was such a hot day!" Or, "The day didn't start out right—I overslept." We'd rather talk about the circumstances than what we did. It's tough to face our failures. But if the heart is going to be cleansed, we have to face our sin honestly.

2. Confession means naming our sins accurately

Naming our sins is a good way to face them. To help us think about this, let me create an imaginary scene.

Suppose that I came to your church to preach. Your minister introduces me, and in an off-the-cuff attempt at humor, he says, "Let's see what this hick from Ohio has to say to us." I don't see the humor in his comment, and I get so upset that I say publicly, "If that's what you think of me, I'll just go back to Ohio!" And I storm out of your church. As I stride down the aisle, I stomp on the minister's foot as I go by. Halfway back to Ohio I decide that what I did wasn't very nice, and I need to clear it up. If I return to your congregation to clear things up, how do I name what I did?

I want to attempt to explain how to name our sins specifically. I'm not intending to say that you have to go through a particular procedure or you won't be cleansed. The attitude of your heart toward your sin is the most important element of your confession. Are you truly penitent? But sometimes, a person will name his sin just to get people off his back. Will that bring cleansing if his heart is not really sorry and he has no intention of leaving the sin? True brokenness is what counts most, but at the same time, accuracy and thoroughness in naming our sins is very helpful in clearing up wrongdoing.

Naming our sins is embarrassing, of course. It makes us feel bad because we know we have failed and done wrong, and now we have to take responsibility for that wrong. Although our natural tendency is to shirk responsibility, we receive a blessing when we are willing to name our sins accurately.

Before I describe how to name our sins, I want to share a quick story about the power of confession. For years, I taught at a winter Bible school. One year a young man came to Bible school who had been there the previous year. When he came the second year, he told me, "One of the reasons I came to Bible School this year is so I can make a confession. When I was here before, I was involved in doing some things against the rules. I want to be able to name those things to the students. I've learned there is power in confession. I have such freedom when I confess my sins." And he did. Early in the term, he took an opportunity to speak to the student body. He said because this was the place where he had broken the rules, he wanted to confess them here as well. I thought, This young man has learned something that we need to pay attention to!

So, what does it mean to confess? The Greek word translated "confess" is made up of two parts—homo is the first part and logeo is the second part. Homo means "same" and logeo means "to speak" or "to say." So, "same to speak" or "same say" would be the two word parts put together. It literally means to "say the same thing." To confess means to say the same thing, or to say exactly how things are.

If I want cleansing from my sin, I need to say exactly what I did.

Let's look at my earlier scenario with my anger and stomping on the minister's toe. To confess my sin, I need to think about three dimensions.

- Fruit: what I actually did. I stomped on his toe. But fruit is a result of something deeper—it grew from a source.
- Root: why did I do that? What motivated my action? It was anger and wounded pride. The deeper condition of the heart produced the fruit of action.

- Effect: how did it affect others? My action hurt someone else.

Sometimes people want to clear things up, so they make a quick and glossed-over confession, and then go on believing it is all taken care of. If I stomped your toe and later came back and said to you, "I'm sorry for getting so excited the other day," how would you feel about forgiving me? If you are a kind and generous person, you might graciously forgive. But you likely would notice that I didn't really name what I did, and that I actually made it sound less hurtful than it was. I did not "say the same thing."

Now, I am not saying that if a person doesn't name his sin exactly right, he won't be forgiven. If his heart is truly penitent, God will hear him. But I'm suggesting there is freedom in being specific and accurate in naming our sin. To confess means to say the same thing.

But before I confess my action (the fruit), I really ought to do some heart work. This action came from something deeper within me. What would be within me that would cause me to stomp on a person's toe?

Furthermore, to look at the whole picture, I should consider what are the effects of my sin? Most of the sins we commit affect others. It causes complications in their lives. If I stomped on a minister's toe, how would that affect him? He would not only have a sore toe, but he would probably struggle with bad feelings. He would be thinking about what a bad spirit I showed, how wrong it was to abort the meeting that way, and how my anger affected the people in his congregation. He would be struggling with more than just a sore toe. He would have a heavy heart.

So, if I really want to clear myself, what should I

do? First, I should open my heart to God and allow Him to show me what conditions in my heart motivated me to do what I did. If I don't deal with the root issue, there is no assurance that it won't happen again. You can pick off the fruit, but it will grow back again if the root is still there. But when I really open my heart to God, He can show me the pride from which my action came. I am then convicted of the pride in my heart as well as how it found expression and I beg God for mercy. "Lord, please cleanse me from this pride, and forgive me for stomping on that man's foot!" But there's more. As I consider what I did, I begin to think about how the minister may have struggled as a result of my action. I realize I hurt him not only physically, but in deeper ways. My rudeness created tension, made an awkward situation for the congregation, and likely caused trouble and wrong attitudes in people's hearts.

Now imagine the difference it would make for this minister and his congregation if I would go to them and say, "God has been convicting me of my pride and selfish anger. My reaction—stomping on your foot— was carnal and immature and wrong. I'm sure you struggled in the next days with what I did. I know that was an awful way to end a meeting, and I'm sure it hurt both you and your people. Would you forgive me?"

Such a confession is both accurate and thorough. It assures people that I have faced the root issues, that I have honestly faced my wrong actions, and that I also considered the effects on others.

There are a number of good results from that kind of confession. One of them is that I obtain freedom. I have freedom in my heart because I have dealt with my pride. I have freedom from guilt by confessing my sin, and I can experience the cleansing of God. An accurate and thorough confession will also enable others to release me. The minister as well as the congregation finds it far easier to forgive when they see that I have been thorough in dealing with my sin.

Of course, when people sin against us and ask for forgiveness, we are called to forgive them. My attempt to show how to confess our sins is not intended to become a way of analyzing confessions. We are all called to forgive even when the confession is not worded exactly right. My point is to show the freedom and cleansing we can have when we accurately say the same thing as what actually happened.

I believe that sometimes the reason we continue to struggle with the same sins over and over is because we have not really confessed them the way the Bible calls us to. When we gloss over what we have done, we are hiding our sin, not confessing it. When we look only at what we did and don't deal with the underlying motivations, we may clear up an incident, but we don't necessarily do what it takes to avoid the same thing from happening again. And when we don't acknowledge the effects of our sin, we can make it more difficult for others to forgive us—they don't have the assurance that we really understand what we did.

I sometimes work with men who struggle with anger and I find that their children are hurting as a result of their father's anger. In fact the whole family is falling apart as a result of the father's anger. Everyone else in the family is aware of the problem, but the father has a hard time naming his sin. When I ask if there is a problem with anger, the others do the talking and the man just sits there. When I question him directly, he says, "Well sometimes I do get a little excited."

Now, for me, the word "excited" has a much nicer ring to it than "angry." When I get excited, I'm usually joyful! You see how easily we try to make our sin not look so bad, to make it look better than it really is. It is tough for human beings to "say the same thing" about their sin—to name it accurately. If you want to be cleansed from sin, name your sin. Cleansing happens as a result of being honest with God, with ourselves, and with others.

Do you enjoy being clean?

I love to look into the faces of those who have just been cleansed of their sins. It is a tremendous joy! One of my favorite psalms is Psalm 34. This is a psalm of David and in verse five he says, "They looked unto him and were lightened: and their faces were not ashamed." When we turn to God, our faces become radiant! I have seen people who have been broken by sin and when they honestly begin to name their sins, the tears begin to flow down their faces. Then I love to look into their faces! Their faces become radiant! The shame is gone! The masks are removed. They are not hiding. They've been cleansed by the blood of Christ and they know it and love it.

Many years ago I was living in northern Minnesota. There was a construction worker I learned to know whose marriage needed help. The man invited me to come to his house and talk. His wife was not there at the time; she actually was living with another man. They had three young children, and they were in the middle of a divorce. Their home was a relational and financial wreck!

This family had come into town in response to a

huge industrial expansion at the paper mill in International Falls. Many people had moved into the area to help work on the project. He was making good money and was putting in a lot of overtime. In just a year's time, he had made over $50,000, which was a good salary for that time. They had payments on a house as well as payments on a van. In spite of his good wage, they were having trouble keeping up with their payments. They loved to go to bars in the evening and dance. They would leave their children with babysitters. Of course, there was flirting going on in those places, and his wife had picked up another boyfriend.

The first time I sat down with him, I listened to his story and found what a mess he was in. I decided I needed to let him know from the start a few things about me too. First, I told him I am a Christian, and I believe the Bible. I made it clear that my counsel and direction for him would be coming from the Word of God. I also wanted him to know I believe what Jesus said about marriage: "What God has joined together, let not man put asunder" (Mark 10:9). I told him I could not counsel him to get a divorce because that is not God's way to resolve marriage problems. He said, "That's what I want—I want God's way."

I asked him if he attended church, and he said he used to but that hadn't been there in quite a while. I shared with him that the most important relationship he has is not with his wife but with God. I told him I can help him only to the extent that he was willing to work on that relationship. We could talk about his marriage, but where he was with God was the biggest issue in his life and the starting point for moving ahead. I took the time to explain the Gospel to him. I told him that we are sinners and that need a Savior because "The wages of sin death" (Romans 6:23). I left some tracts with him and told him we could talk again.

The next day he called me and wanted to talk again. He said he wanted to share what had happened to him during the night. We got together, and he related to me what had happened. "My wife went to the bar like normal, and I stayed home with the children. It was bedtime and I was alone. I went to bed, but I couldn't sleep. About midnight, I got up and read those tracts you left. I knew from when I attended church before that God wants us to confess our sins. I wasn't sure what to do but I knelt down and began to confess all the sins I could think of at that time. I told God everything. I went back to bed—." He paused and then said, "This is going to sound funny, but I just couldn't quit smiling!"

Confession brings cleansing—and it feels so good to have a clean heart. I don't know if he named everything accurately, but he understood the need for confession. He realized that he needed to face his sins and name them to God.

His situation was not easy. I was able to sit down with his wife later, and I tried to explain the way of salvation to her too, but I felt like I was up against a brick wall. I could tell I was not communicating with her. What I tried to say was just not registering. I never did get through to her, but her husband, Brian, continued to grow. It was incredible some of the ways God worked in his life. Not everything got worked out right away but confessing his sins was the way he started in the right direction. Brian was a changed man. I watched him relate to his wife and children, and the difference cleansing had made was amazing. The heart is cleansed through confession.

The heart is cleansed through repentance

In Acts 3:19 Peter says, "Repent ye therefore, and be converted, that your sins may be blotted out, when the times of refreshing shall come from the presence of the Lord." Repentance is an important part of cleansing. Repentance involves a turning from. The literal idea is a turning away from, but it is accompanied with sorrow for what has been done.

For Brian, it was not just a matter of naming his sins, but there also needed to be a turning away from his sins. Some of that happened immediately, but there was also ongoing repentance and change. He had habits—I didn't focus on those initially. Instead I focused on where his heart was. I encouraged him to cultivate a relationship with God.

Some of the other people in our congregation interacted with Brian as well. My fellow-minister took him to listen to a preacher holding meetings some distance from our hometown. On the way as they were talking, Brian asked him to stop. When they stopped, Brian reached in his pocket and pulled out a snuff can. He opened the door, got out, and threw it as hard as he could into the woods. He said, "Now, I'm done with that!" Then he got back in the car and said, "Let's keep going." Ironically, my fellow-minister had not been talking about tobacco at all.

Turning away from the old life is both immediate and ongoing. We make a big turn-around when we come to Christ. But as we walk with Him, we may become aware of hidden attitudes in our heart or practices in our life that are not pleasing to Him.

Sometimes it is not turning from wrong ways to right ways so much as turning from common ways to better ways. We may not be aware of those things initially, but as we turn away from the world, we should also be turning toward God. With the "away" direction, there should always be a "toward" direction. Repentance is not just giving up something; it is also taking on something else. Cleansing involves getting rid of things in our lives in order that we can take on new and better things

We are cleansed through fellowship with God

Going back to 1 John 1, in verses 5-6 we read, "This then is the message which we have heard of him, and declare unto you that God is light, and in him is no darkness at all. If we say that we have fellowship with him and walk in darkness, we lie and do not the truth." Now notice verse 7: "But if we walk in the light, as he is in the light, we have fellowship one with another, and the blood of Jesus Christ his Son cleanseth us from all sin." Here we see that cleansing comes through fellowship. As we turn away from sin, we are leaving what is defiling and turning toward the One who is holy. In fellowship with Him, our lives are cleansed. There is a getting rid of old ways and an embracing of ways that are holy and true. It is like leaving the darkness and entering the light. It is like getting rid of rags and putting on clean clothes.

Jesus said in John 15:3, "Now ye are clean through the word which I have spoken unto you." Walking with Him results in cleansing. Walking with God is involving Him in all of my life. Part of the walking is listening to Him speak.

Listen to Him speak

In John 1:1, Jesus is called "the Word." That word is logos, the noun form of the word part we talked about earlier (logeo). Jesus is the speech, the word, the saying, the great Message from God to us. He is what God is speaking to humanity. Jesus is that Word. When you walk with Jesus, He will say things to you. You cannot walk with the true Jesus without hearing things. When we walk with Jesus, then, we have to keep our ears open because he will speak. It is an integral part of who Jesus is to communicate and to say things. We are cleansed in fellowship with Him because He speaks words that get rid of filth and give us purity, righteousness, and holiness.

The heart needs to be cleansed because it has absorbed sinfulness. The longer we live in selfishness and sin, the more selfish and sinful our hearts become. This absorption of sin calls for cleansing.

There is an initial cleansing as well as on-going cleansing. Through the blood of Christ, we are cleansed of our sin—our record is clear. Then there is on-going cleansing through the Word that He speaks to us. Ephesians 5:26 says, "That he might sanctify and cleanse it with the washing of water by the word" (speaking of Christ and the church). The Word operates in us like a washing action.

If you place a sponge in a mud puddle, what's going to happen? Dirt doesn't just get on the sponge; it gets in the sponge. The sponge absorbs the dirt. Our problem with sin is that it's not just something attached to us, but something in us.

Now, how do you cleanse a dirty sponge? Do you just take it out of the mud? No. Of course, you have to start there—that's like repentance. But the sponge needs more than being taken out of the mud. The best way to cleanse the dirt that's in the sponge is to put the sponge under running water and then wring it and wring it until the water going out of the sponge is the same color as the water going into it.

That's the kind of cleansing that happens in us when we are in fellowship with God. The word that God speaks into our lives is pure and clear, and He wants what is coming out of our lives to be the same quality as the word coming in. The cleansing that happens in fellowship with Him is a blessed cleansing, but it also involves a certain amount of wringing. When God squeezes your heart, don't be too quick to say, "Please stop!" Instead, ask Him to purge you by the experience, so that the outflow from your life is pure and clear. This cleansing happens in an ongoing acquaintance with God, and it is a joy to experience.

The things God cleanses out of our lives when we are in fellowship with Him are not taken away because God wants to deprive us but because He wants to fill us. He wants to give us something better. With our sin-clouded eyes, we tend to think that when God is asking us to give up something, it will take away our happiness. The truth is that God never asks anybody to give up something that He does not replace it with something far better. That's a part of the cleansing. Cleansing involves more than just getting rid of dirt. It includes taking in, receiving, putting on something better. This is part of the holiness and righteousness of God which we receive in fellowship with Him.

So, how is the heart cleansed? We are cleansed by confession—by naming our sins accurately, by saying what is exactly true about them. We are cleansed by repentance—by turning around in sorrow from the ways of selfishness and sin and turning toward the ways of God. We are also cleansed through fellowship with God—by walking with Him, hearing what He has to say, and allowing His words to bring new life into our hearts so that the outflow of our lives—our words, actions, attitudes, plans, and decisions—are Christ-like and bring glory to God. Thus, in fellowship with God, our hearts are cleansed.

Chapter

7

Heart Change

One of the things God wants to do in our hearts is to purify them. Sometimes people think of becoming a Christian as merely a pardon from God—forgiveness of sins. I believe our sins are forgiven when we come to God through faith in Christ, but I don't think that is all that happens.

A number of surveys have been taken in recent years in the U.S. asking Christian people how they actually lived. The surveys have found that the lifestyle of churchgoers was little different from the lifestyle of non-Christians! In fact, I heard recently the divorce rate among evangelical Christians is nine percent higher than the national average, and the divorce rate among Pentecostal groups is eleven percent higher than the national average. I'm not trying to knock any denomination, but that is a pathetic indictment on Western Christianity—I say that with sorrow. If becoming a Christian does not result in heart change that translates into changed living, then I do not see how we can claim we have come to Jesus Christ. God is a life changer. He does more than forgive our sins.

As we read the New Testament, we find Jesus changed people. And the early church expected believers to have a change of life. Paul wrote, "Therefore, if any man be in Christ, he is a new creature: old things are passed away; behold, all things are become new" (2 Corinthians 5:17). Not one of the New Testament writers teach that believers will live perfect lives, that we will never sin; but they do teach that there will be change and growth in a believer's life. The analogy of growth is used over and over. So, when we talk about change, we are talking about something that it is an integral part of Christianity. It is a given. Change happens in those who actually meet and welcome Jesus into their hearts. John wrote, "Whosoever abideth in him sinneth not: whosoever sinneth hath not seen him, neither known him" (1 John 3:16). "Sinneth" indicates continuous action. The person who lives in Jesus does not practice or continue to live in sin. The NIV says, "No one who lives in Him keeps on sinning." There's going to be a change. It doesn't say such a person will never commit a sin, but he does not go on living in sin.

The Scriptures teach that no one who is born of God will continue to sin because God's seed remains in him, and he cannot go on sinning because he has been born of God. If your life is continuing the same way it was before you received Jesus and if it is not distinguishable from the people who don't know God, then you have not changed. There has not been a transformation of heart.

Remember in the first session we learned that the heart is the source of all living? Our thoughts, words, and actions come out of our heart. If we want to change our thoughts, words, and actions, then, what has to change? The heart has to change. Transformation of the heart: that's what we are talking about.

The heart is changed through acquaintance with God

The heart is transformed as we learn to know God in increasing ways. In 2 Corinthians 3:18 we read, "But we all, with open face beholding as in a glass [or mirror] the glory of the Lord, are changed...." The word "changed" here is a powerful word. In the Greek language it is metamorphoo. Scientists have drawn from that word to describe the life-change that happens when a caterpillar turns into a butterfly. That's a transformation. The life-change that happens in the believer is likewise a change from within. We are metamorphosed into the image of God "from glory to glory even as by the Spirit of the Lord" (2 Corinthians 3:18).

This is the point I want to spend the most time on because it is foundational to all heart change. We must learn to know God. Later we will talk about other things that are involved in change, but I want to start by listing Scriptures that speak about this.

In John 17:3 Jesus is praying, and He said, "This is life eternal, that they might know thee the only true God, and Jesus Christ, whom thou hast sent." The Greek word for knowledge is gnosis which means an acquaintance through experience. It is not simply an informational knowing about someone, but an acquaintance that is learned through experience.

I ask my audiences sometimes, how well do you know me? If you have met me and I have told you a bit about myself, you could say you know John Coblentz. Do you know where I live? Do you know my wife's name? How many children do I have? What kind of person am I when I first wake up in the morning? What is my favorite meat? Do I tend to stock up on a good deal or buy as I go? Do I tend to buy quality products and pay more, or do I try to get by as cheaply as possible?

Most of my audience cannot get beyond the first couple of informational questions. They know about me, but they don't really know me. But if you talked to my wife, she could tell you the answer to all those questions because she lives with me. She is acquainted through experience.

So when we try to understand what it means to know God, we are talking about acquaintance with God on a deep level. Such acquaintance with God is life-changing. You cannot spend time with God without being changed.

The Apostle Peter says some astounding things about knowing God. "Simon Peter, a servant and an apostle of Jesus Christ, to them that have obtained like precious faith with us through the righteousness of God and our Savior Jesus Christ: Grace and peace be multiplied unto you through the knowledge of God, and of Jesus our Lord" (2 Peter 1:1, 2). Through acquaintance with God, Peter says, grace and peace are multiplied to us. Do you know what grace is? It is more than just good feelings. Grace is the favor of God that makes His resources available to us. Grace is what enables us. It is actions of God's favor in our behalf.

I don't know Bill Gates personally. I know of him. When I say Bill Gates, what comes to your mind? Microsoft. Money. He's known for his wealth. Suppose I learn to know him in such a way that I have his favor—not just his feelings of goodwill, but the kind of favor that he makes his resources available to me. Bill Gates is married. Suppose he has a child. And suppose one day I save his child from terrible death. He looks into my finances and decides that I could use some help. He tells me that he is going to make his resources available to me. He creates a bank account for me to draw from whenever I need it. He tells me he will put five million dollars in to begin with and encourages me to draw from it! He could do that, couldn't he? That's not just doing a favor—that is showing the kind of favor toward someone that makes your resources available.

God's grace is His favor and goodwill that makes His resources available to us. Peter says, grace is multiplied to us through acquaintance with God. People learn to know God by spending time with Him, by walking with Him, by living with Him—He is the rewarder of those who diligently seek Him (Hebrews 11:6). God's grace is multiplied to those who become acquainted with Him. Do you know why people don't have the grace and power to live in this world today? It is because they don't know God. Grace and peace are multiplied to us through acquaintance with Him.

Peter goes on to say (v.3), "According as his divine power hath given unto us all things that pertain unto life and godliness, through the knowledge of Him that hath called us to glory and virtue." Everything we need for living and for godliness is given to us through the knowledge of God. I cannot overemphasize the importance and the blessing of learning to know Him. How did I learn to know my wife? How did she learn to know me? We learned to know each other by spending time with each other, by living life together. We live in continual acquaintance with each other.

Learning to know a fellow human being always results in a certain amount of disappointment. You can like a person ever so much, but when you learning to know the person, eventually you learn things that are uncomplimentary. Usually, dating doesn't get us very far in acquaintance. We think it does because it stirs a lot of deep feelings. We get to the point we think we can't live without this person any longer— and so we get married. Then, the real acquaintance begins. Perhaps that is overstating it a bit, but many times we are rather blind in dating. We don't really see. Once we live with the person, we start to know him or her in ways we didn't know before.

Acquaintance is like waking full circle around a person's life. Eventually we get around on the "back side" and see that in the early days of acquaintance the best foot was always forward. Hopefully, it's not too horrifying what we discover back there. All of us eventually find out that there are imperfections in each other's lives—things we didn't know. For example, you didn't know how she relates first thing in the morning. Or you didn't know how he responds when someone cheats him out of a dollar. When you get around on the back side, you learn about those things.

Acquaintance with God will also bring surprises. There are times we learn to know things about God that are disturbing. Some things about God we cannot fully understand. We struggle and grapple with them. Job, for example, faced some things about God that almost unsettled him. And Job was a righteous man. He had to learn that God can allow intense difficulties and struggles and He is still good. Job had trouble accepting that God can allow His children to suffer. He struggled and struggled with the silence of God when he was hurting. That was something he could not understand about God. God did eventual speak and Job accepted what God had to say. He actually clapped his hand over his mouth and said, "I'm sorry I said a word; I wish I hadn't spoken!"

When you face something in your acquaintance with God and find yourself struggling, my encouragement to you is to just keep going. Keep learning to know God and you will learn the things that enable you to live and that enable you to be godly. Eventually, you will thank God for who He is and beg Him never to change! You will learn to know Him by walking through those difficult things with Him.

There are some beautiful things said about people in the Bible. I pray that at least one of those things could be said about me when I am finished with my life. "Noah walked with God" (Genesis 6:9). It would bring hallelujahs to my soul if that could be on my tombstone, and if it would accurately capture my life! "Enoch walked with God" (Genesis 5:22). "David was a man after God's own heart" (Acts 13:22). "Abraham was the friend of God" (James 2:23). What would be the caption of your life? If we could capture your life in one sentence, would it have anything to do with knowing God? Knowing God gives us everything that is necessary for life and godliness. It is through learning to know Him that our hearts are changed.

Peter says more. "Whereby are given unto us exceeding great and precious promises: that by these ye might be partakers of the divine nature, having escaped the corruption that is in the world through lust" (v.4). Learning to know God gives us great and precious promises. It enables us to become sharers and partakers of His divine nature.

In verses 5-8 Peter says, "And beside this, giving all diligence, add to your faith virtue; and to virtue knowledge; and to knowledge temperance; and to temperance patience; and to patience godliness; and to godliness brotherly kindness; and to brotherly kindness charity. For if these things be in you, and abound, they make you that ye shall neither be barren nor unfruitful in the knowledge of our Lord Jesus Christ." What is he saying? He is saying that when we know God, good things keep happening inside us. Faith, virtue, knowledge, temperance, patience, godliness, brotherly kindness, and charity—these things will be growing in you. Not growing in meager measure, but growing in abundance as you learn to know God.

Learning to know God is a lifelong process. It goes on and on and on. I've known the Lord for many years and one of the prayers in my heart is to know Him better.

Two ladies stood by the shore of the ocean for the

first time in their lives. Their jaws fell open as they gazed over the seascape before them. Finally, one of the ladies said, "Look at all that water!" And the other lady remarked, "Yes, and that's just the top of it!"

I've been on the ocean and flown over the ocean. It is incredible to imagine that I can be flying five miles above the ocean surface, and in certain spots I could go just as far below the surface of the ocean and not hit the bottom!

Can you grasp that faltering analogy? Acquaintance with God is like exploring the ocean. Sometimes I feel like I'm simply wading in the shallows, and I want to get to the depths where I'm way over my head.

One of my concerns for conservative Anabaptist groups is our complacent spirituality. I say that with deep compassion. We have learned to measure spirituality superficially, and we say we are good Christians because we don't do this or we don't do that. We require that everyone in our church looks nice. And we think we are good Christians! But how does God measure spirituality?

If God measured you by your acquaintance with Him, how would you measure up? Are you into the ocean? Sometimes I am too careless about my acquaintance with God. I find it helpful to fellowship with other people whose passion it is to know Him. It has also been helpful for me to read books by people who share the same passion.

One book that has helped deepen my acquaintance with God is A.W. Tozer's book, The Knowledge of the Holy. That was one of the first books that really took me into His acquaintance in deep and passionate ways. I loved that book, and I enjoyed his writings on the holiness, goodness, justice, and other attributes of

God. Recently, I revisited that book, reading a chapter a day, meditating on it as a way to refresh my heart. I love to read the Psalms for the same reason. They open God to me and guide me into deeper acquaintance with Him.

I don't know how you go about learning to know God, but I want to encourage you to be passionate about it. Learning to know God and Jesus Christ is eternal life. Your heart will come to life by interacting, walking, and fellowshipping with Him. It is inevitable that if you spend time with God on a regular basis, you will be changed. You won't be able to experience those changes any other way. He does all things well, and He does it well in the 21st century. God still changes people.

When we are being changed by God, we love to meet other people who are learning to know Him. There is instantaneous compatibility. I love to see the changes God makes in the lives of others. He changes their heart immediately! I've seen people who are against God one day, and the very next day they are saying things that are wise and astounding. They begin to reflect a totally different perspective and all that happened to them was they met God. Putting God back on the throne of their heart gave them wisdom. They start saying things that only the day before they could not say!

I remember a young man at Bible school who came for three weeks. The longer he was there, the more miserable he became. We had a concluding music program at the end of the term, and he asked me if he could do something that no student had ever asked to do. He asked to go home before the program! All the other students I had ever known looked forward to the closing program, but not him. He wanted out of there. The next-to-last day of the term, we did a recording. He said he was sick and spent the time back in his dorm. During the recording, I was in my office, and finally this young man came to see me. He said, "John, could I talk to you?" We went into the prayer room and he began to cry. He told me, "I am so miserable! I have a girlfriend back home that my parents don't approve of. I have been resisting them, but since I am here at Bible school I have been miserable! I don't want to give in to God." We talked for a while, and finally, he said he wants to surrender his heart to God. We prayed. He asked God to forgive him for his stubbornness. He was a different person. And he began to talk totally different from the way he had talked just the day before.

Even though there is initial change when we meet God, don't think for a moment that the instant change is all there is! It is a lifelong process. Continue to pursue Him and allow Him to shape you into His likeness.

"But we all, with open face beholding as in a glass the glory of the Lord, are changed into the same image from glory to glory" (2 Corinthians 3:18). We are transformed from the inside into His same image from glory to glory.

The heart is changed through truth

Jesus said that the heart is changed through truth. In John 17:17, He is praying and He says, "Sanctify them through thy truth: thy word is truth." His Word is an expression of who He is. When we learn to know God, we will hear truth from Him, and the heart will be changed. "Sanctify" means to set apart and make holy for God's purposes. Hearts are set apart for God through truth.

When we sin, we embrace ruinous ideas. A major tactic of the enemy is to infect the mind with twisted ideas so we think in ways that actually ruin us. Do you remember that from one of the previous sessions? Sin darkens the mind. I shared with you some of the stupid thinking we get into when we don't know God. The ideas that people will live by when they neither know God nor have a desire to are ridiculous! "In whom the god of this world hath blinded the minds of them which believe not, lest the light of the glorious gospel of Christ, who is the image of God, should shine unto them" (2 Corinthians 4:4).

Have you found yourself sometimes believing lies? The big struggle is often whether we will continue to believe these lies or accept the truth. Even after we are Christians, we are given truth that shows we still have wrong ideas. We go through new experiences as believers, and sometimes we develop wrong concepts. Job, through the tragedies he faced, developed the idea that he would like to argue his case before God. He wanted to have a mediator with one hand on God's shoulder and the other on himself. When God finally spoke, Job was sorry he had said those things. God doesn't have to give an account to His creatures! He knows what He is doing.

Other times, our ideas are a carry-over from the old life. We change, but we also need to continue to change and be sanctified through God's truth. We need this continued exposure to truth. In Psalm 119:160, the psalmist says to God what Jesus said: Thy word is truth." We need to expose ourselves to the Word of God so it can change us.

Let's revisit my prior story about the rivalry I had in my heart. When God showed me my heart, I asked Him to change me. I wrote out my sin specifically and faced what was going on in my heart. Then I found verses that had to do with my struggle, verses that exposed the sin of rivalry and also verses that showed the way of love and humility—putting others first, not trying to outperform them. I read and reread those verses because they applied to the specific areas that needed to change. I found this was powerful in changing my heart.

When I was a boy, I did a lot of running and jumping. I also did a lot of falling. Once I tore a tooth out of my mouth, and often I wiped out on my hands and knees in gravel. I remember one time in particular when I really tore up my hands. My mother was a believer in Merthiolate. (You older folks will remember that red stuff that burns like fire.) She believed that if you had scrapes, you had to have the red stuff. I still remember how I quivered while it burned, and the awful sense of relief I had when it finally quit.

Now, suppose I have these scrapes on my hands and my mother gets the Merthiolate. Where is she going to put it? I could tell her, "Mom, put it on my head!" She could dump the whole bottle on my head and it would not do any good. She always put it exactly where the problem was.

When we have problems in our lives, the first thing to do is to confess them to God. When we confess, He forgives us. But that doesn't mean everything is taken care of. Next, I go to the Scriptures, find exactly what God says about that need, and apply it exactly to the problem area. I find verses on pride and humility if that is the problem. I write them out and I read those verses. It burns as it penetrates the heart. When you apply God's word specifically to your heart where your needs are, your heart will be changed! I have been blessed over and over seeing how this happens in people's lives.

Sometimes when we have a need in our lives, we open our Bibles and begin reading wherever it falls open. Then we hope we get better. That's like dumping a little Merthiolate on one arm and hoping it fixes a problem on the other arm! You didn't apply it specifically where the need was. If you have a specific problem, apply God's Word to that specific area and let it do its work in you. Jesus' prayer to the Father was, "Sanctify them through thy truth; thy word is truth" (John 17:17).

When I am feeling proud, I am thinking false things about myself and I have a false sense of importance. When I read the Word of God, it changes the way I think. The lie I believed about myself—that I deserve a certain amount of respect—is changed into my new thought—if I got what I truly deserve, I would run from it! I don't want to get what I deserve! Do any of you want to get what you deserve? Absolutely not! We want mercy!

Do you see how the perspective changes by going to the Scriptures? By exposure to truth, we discover the lies we've been thinking when we are proud or angry or lustful. We discover that we have been entertaining ideas in our heart that are contrary to the Word of God. That's why we need regular exposure to truth of God's Word. His truth will transform you. If you are struggling with something, go to the Scriptures. Meditate on the truth of God's Word.

When I do this personally, I read over those verses often enough until the Spirit of God begins to speak through them to my specific need. I like to write down the things He says to me. Sometimes I rewrite the verses to apply them to my specific situation as the Spirit illuminates them to me. What's that doing? It helps me change the way I think. It does a work of grace in my heart.

The heart is affected by circumstances

Circumstances do affect us. Some days we experience reverses and things don't go the way we planned. Some days we learn things about people who are close to us and it affects us deeply. It could be a family member, a relative, or a church member. We might learn, for example, that they are going backward spiritually. It hurts us. Or maybe we learn that they said something unkind about us or misrepresented us. They might have said something to someone else that's not true. Does that affect us? Yes.

Now, we noted earlier that the lasting effect on our heart has more to do with how we respond to those circumstances than the circumstances themselves. So how should we respond to these kinds of experiences? Initially, we may feel disappointed. We will feel sorrow, or even anger about something that has happened. We may think, "This is totally unfair!" But where should we go from there? How should we actually live?

I believe we have an interactive relationship with life and growth. When it comes to change—to living and growing—we are continually interacting with life. I am so grateful that the Scriptures teach us something more than determinism. If we believed in determinism, we would assume that we are shaped by whatever happens to us and we simply are the product of all the experiences we've had in life. Thankfully, that is not true. Life is not determined for us—otherwise there would be no hope of us being involved in change.

The reality is that God not only gives us the opportunity to make right choices, but He also gives us the responsibility to do so. That is why two people can experience nearly identical circumstances, and one of them becomes bitter and the other one becomes beautiful. What is the difference? The difference is determined by how they responded to those circumstances. That is the interactive relationship we have with life.

Without effort we are always becoming more like ourselves. But when we make right choices by learning to know God, we are becoming more and more like He wants us to be—like Himself. We take on the kind of person that God has intended us to become.

And God uses the experiences we have in life to give us opportunities to grow, to deepen, to become more compassionate, to cultivate meaningful relationships, to learn to pray, to become more aware of His purposes. So the heart truly is affected by circumstances, and in those circumstances, we have the continued challenge to become better people.

The heart is changed by love

In writing to the Ephesians, Paul talks about change and spiritual growth. He says," But speaking the truth in love, may grow up into him in all things"

(4:15). Love is life changing.

Our encounter with love usually starts with receiving love. There are many, many twisted and warped people living in our world today. The first thing that needs to happen in the lives of those people is to be loved. They can receive God's love through God's people. That's one of the challenges of living the Christian life in a wicked world—there are people around us who need God, whose lives are a mess. They need to experience love—most of them have no idea there is a God who loves them.

Of course, that's not all that needs to happen. If people stay in that stage, they will be little more than sponges. They will take anything others give them, but they won't grow into givers.

Love given completes the transformation. We are changed as we receive love, but God's intent is that the love received turns into love given back. "We love him because He first loved us" (1 John 4:19). And so, first, we receive His love, and then we give it back to Him and we are changed in the process.

Not only that, but in that love relationship with God, we begin to give it out to other people. Love given transforms people's lives. Somehow, love puts the heart back in order again. As we exercise love, as we learn to live in love, our hearts will be changed more and more into the image of God. "God so loved the world that He gave..." (John 3:16). God is a giving God. He sends His rain on the just and on the unjust" (Matthew 5:45). He gives to the deserving and to the undeserving. He is a giving kind of God and He does it because He is love.

If you want to become like God, if you want your heart to be changed, learn to think about the good of others. It is so easy to live selfish lives. Do you want to be changed into a selfless person? Learn to think about others. Give yourself to working for their best interest. That is a change in heart.

The last three points we have looked at are only outgrowths of the first one—the heart is changed through acquaintance with God. That's the number one heart change. We think about truth, we think the heart being affected by circumstances, and we think about love—in reality these are just different dimensions of learning to know God.

The heart being changed through love is just an extension of a heart being changed through acquaintance with God. As we learn to know Him, our hearts are changed by His love, and we become loving in the pattern of God. We are demonstrating to others what we have experienced from Him. The two best therapies for people today whose lives are laden with problems are first, to learn to know God and second, to give themselves to loving other people. It's good therapy. It helps depression and all sorts of other problems as people learn to know God and learn to love others.

My prayer is that you can come away from this discussion with a heart for God, with a heart that is yearning to know God and is set on knowing Him. If you are going to have a heart for God, you must cut out some things that others do. It takes time. If you are really going to know Him, there will be sacrifices you will need to make. In some ways it really isn't a sacrifice because we get so much more than what we give up! If you turn toward God and seek Him, He will reward you. May the Lord draw you to Himself, and someday may we meet together around the throne of our God!